Defending the Borders

The Role of Border and Immigration Control

Defending the Borders
The Role of Border and Immigration Control

Other titles in the Lucent Library of Homeland Security

Deterring and Investigating Attack
Hunting Down the Terrorists
Responding to Attack
A Vulnerable America

THE
LUCENT
LIBRARY OF
HOMELAND
SECURITY

Defending the Borders

The Role of Border and Immigration Control

Gail B. Stewart

LUCENT
BOOKS®

THOMSON
—✴—
GALE

San Diego • Detroit • New York • San Francisco • Cleveland • New Haven, Conn. • Waterville, Maine • London • Munich

LIBRARY OF CONGRESS CATALOGING-IN-PUBLICATION DATA

Stewart, Gail B., 1949–
    Defending the borders: the role of border and immigration control / by Gail B. Stewart.
    p. cm. — (Lucent library of homeland security)
Includes bibliographical references and index.
Summary: Dissolution of the INS, economic and political impact of U.S. sea and land bor-
ders, changing immigration patterns and the future of U.S. borders.
    ISBN 1-59018-376-2 (hb)
    1. War on Terrorism, 2001—Juvenile literature. 2. Terrorism—United States—Prevention—
Juvenile literature. 3. Border patrols—United States—Juvenile literature. 4. Terrorism—
Prevention—Juvenile literature. 5. Terrorists—Juvenile literature. [1. War on terrorism,
2001– 2. Terrorism—Prevention. 3. Border patrols. 4. Terrorists.] I. Title. II. Series.
    HV6432.S743 2004
    973.931—dc21
                                                                        2003010074

Printed in the United States of America

Contents

Foreword

Stunned by the terrorist attacks of September 11, 2001, millions of Americans clung to President George W. Bush's advice in a September 20 live broadcast speech to "live your lives, and hug your children." His soothing words made an indelible impression on people in need of comfort and paralyzed by fear. Recent history had seen no greater emotional flood than occurred in the days following September 11, as people were united by deep shock and grief and an instinctive need to feel safe.

Searching for safety, a panicked nation urged taking extreme and even absurd measures. Immediately after the attacks, it was suggested that all aircraft passengers be restrained for the duration of flights—better to restrict the movement of all than to risk allowing one dangerous passenger to act. After the attempted bombing of a flight from Paris to Atlanta in December 2001, one *New York Times* columnist even half-seriously suggested starting an airline called Naked Air—"where the only thing you wear is a seat belt." Although such acute fear and paranoia waned as the attacks slipped further into the past, a dulled but enduring desire to overhaul national security remained.

Creating the Department of Homeland Security was one way to allay citizens' panic and fear. Congress has allocated billions to secure the nation's infrastructure, bolster communication channels, and protect precious monuments against terrorist attack. Further funding has equipped emergency responders with state-of-the-art tools such as hazardous-material suits and networked communication systems. Improved databases and intelligence-gathering tools have extended the reach of intelligence agencies, in the effort to ferret out the terrorists hiding among us. Supporters of these programs praised the Bush administration for its attention to security lapses and agreed that in the post–September 11 world, only with tighter security could Americans go about their lives free of fear and reservation.

It did not take long, however, for the sense of national unity and purpose to splinter as people advanced countless ideas for actually achieving that security. As it became evident that ensuring safety meant curtailing Americans' freedom, the price of security became a hotly debated issue. With September 11 now years in the past, and after new wars and aggression waged in its name, it is not clear that the United States is any closer to becoming what many consider impossible: an America immune to attack. As distinguished political science professor Janice Gross Stein maintains, "Military preeminence, no matter how overwhelming, does not buy the United States security from attack, even in its heartland." Whether the invasion of sovereign nations, the deaths of thousands of civilians, and the continued endangerment of American troops have made the world any safer or the United States any less vulnerable to terror is unproved.

All Americans want to feel safe; beyond that basic agreement, however, commonality ends. Thus, how to ensure homeland security, and a myriad of related questions, is one of the most compelling and controversial issues in recent history. The books in this series explore this new chapter in history and examine its successes and challenges. Annotated bibliographies provide readers with ideas for further research, while fully documented primary and secondary source quotations enhance the text. Each book in the series carefully considers a different aspect of homeland security; together they provide students with a wealth of information as well as launching points for further study and discussion.

"What Were We *Doing?*"

The first question people asked when they heard about the terrorist attacks on September 11, 2001, was "who?" Who would do a thing like this, use commercial jetliners full of civilians to kill thousands of other civilians? In the days and weeks following the attacks, as newspapers reported the activities and the elaborate planning of the hijackers, Americans demanded the answer to another question: "How?"

Rick, a city park employee in Minneapolis, remembers hearing the question from almost everyone. People wanted to understand how individuals could enter the country with plans to kill thousands of innocent people—and then walk onto airplanes and carry out those plans. "It was like a mantra, over and over—the 'how coulds,'" he recalls. "I remember thinking, 'My God, what are we doing, letting monsters like that into the United States?'"[1]

Finger-Pointing

As more information came to light after September 11, there was a great deal of finger-pointing among various government agencies. Of special concern was the lack of communication between those who manned the nation's borders and the members of the U.S. intelligence community, who were supposed to have been keeping track of people known to have ties with international terrorism.

Susan, an editor who like many Americans followed the coverage of the terrorist acts very closely, says that she became angry when she learned that at least some of the hijackers were already known terrorists. She remembers,

It was really infuriating when you learn that the FBI or whoever—they knew some of these guys, and what they might be capable of. . . . Yet the people manning the borders didn't get the message, or something, and they let

A police officer patrols the Port of Houston. He is on the lookout for terrorists and other potential threats.

these terrorists in. What I say is, if we can learn from this tragedy, at least one small positive can come out of it. But it makes you rethink everything you ever believed about how strong our nation is when these guys didn't even need to use fake names, and still not one U.S. official caught on. I mean, you tell me—what is going on with the way our borders are manned? What were we *doing*?[2]

That same frustration was felt by government leaders in Washington, D.C., especially because some experts believed the attacks of September 11 were just the beginning—that there were more terrorist cells already in the United States, waiting for the signal to strike again. FBI officials, for instance, admitted that the agency was almost certain that other cells existed in Florida, as well as in the cities of Detroit and Boston.

Based on these concerns, President George W. Bush insisted on a drastic increase in the 2002 federal budget for border security. More than $11 billion was allotted by Congress for updating computers, increasing the number of agents staffing the U.S. borders shared with Canada and Mexico, and increasing the manpower of the U.S. Coast Guard, which is responsible for protecting the coastal borders.

President Bush warned the American people about possible al-Qaeda terrorists already in their midst, weeks after the attacks. "The enemy still wants to hit us," he declared. "And therefore this nation must do everything in our power to prevent it."[3] He added that, hopefully, with a strong effort to tighten the nation's borders, the United States would not only be able to keep out other terrorists, but also any weapons of mass destruction that could be used against the nation.

Chapter One

The End of the INS

The porous state of the nation's borders should not have been much of a surprise to anyone—least of all to the agency responsible for them, the Immigration and Naturalization Service, or INS. At the time of the September 11 attacks, it was one of the fastest-growing agencies in Washington, D.C., yet with an outdated computer system and huge backlog of paperwork, noted Eric Schmitt of the *New York Times*, "the most fouled up."[4]

Part of the problem for the INS was the enormity of its assignment. First, it was in charge of monitoring the 500 million people—approximately 330 million of them noncitizens—who enter the United States each year. Before they can be allowed into the country, they must produce a valid passport along with a visa or other documentation, which gives the INS information to determine how long they can remain in the United States.

The second of the agency's jobs was to provide assistance to immigrants. New residents would need information on citizenship classes, finding jobs, getting health care, and enrolling their children in schools. "There's a lot of confusing bureaucratic red tape for a native-born American who wants to get a loan or something," said Jim, who teaches English to immigrants. "But just think—if it's confusing for us, imagine what it's like for someone who is just learning English, just getting used to this country. The INS is the organization that tries to step in and give immigrants a hand."[5]

An Immigration and Naturalization Service (INS) agent verifies the identity of an immigrant. The INS monitors and provides assistance to the millions of foreigners who enter the United States each year.

Second-guessing

As more information about the attacks came to light, it was clear that the INS had not performed either of its responsibilities very well. Two of the nineteen hijackers had already been identified by international intelligence agencies as terrorists, and their names had been put on border "watch lists." They should never have been allowed into the country, yet they entered and exited border crossings several times over a two-year period. Several other hijackers had entered the United States using stolen or forged passports, which had not been spotted by INS agents. And five of the nineteen men should have been deported by the INS well before September 11, 2001, because their visas had all expired.

James Ziglar, head of the INS, acknowledged that his agency had indeed made mistakes. However, he explained, those mistakes could be traced back to budget shortfalls over the past several years. The agency lacked an adequate number of border inspectors and the INS had neither enough agents nor enough technological support to do the jobs it was expected to do.

Ziglar felt confident that if the INS were given more funds, there would be improvements made—both in maintaining a higher level of border security and in keeping track of the millions of immigrants entering the United States. Although they hoped he was right, some government officials worried that the agency's problems might be too difficult to fix.

"Why Didn't Anyone Speak Up?"

One of the early priorities in the war on terrorism was locating possible cells of terrorists already in the United States. However, if the public believed that the INS would be of any help in tracking down these cells, they soon learned otherwise. INS officials explained that they had no way of checking which immigrants had overstayed their visas, since the agency only recorded the names of people arriving in the country, not leaving. They estimated that there were as many as 3 million foreign visitors, still in the United States, whose visas had expired. Again, the agency blamed budget restrictions and a lack of manpower: The INS had only seventeen hundred agents to locate them. And, explained INS officials, those agents had plenty of other duties—such as locating noncitizen criminals and investigating employers who exploit illegal immigrants. There simply were not enough agents to do all that was asked of them.

The government's admission that the nation's borders were not secure, combined with the fear that there were more terrorists already inside the country, frightened and angered many Americans. Gilda, a graduate student in business affairs at the University of Minnesota, complained that she had the feeling that no one had been taking responsibility for what was a very important job. She said,

> It's like nobody is accountable for their work. . . . How is the system supposed to work, and why haven't we been told about these problems until now, when it's too late? If people had been thinking about how important their jobs were, and they knew that they had no idea where immigrants are at any one moment, why didn't anyone speak up? Did it take thousands of people getting murdered on 9/11 for anyone to care?"[6]

Immigrants stand in line at the INS to register for a new security program created in the wake of the September 11 terrorist attacks.

Cracking Down

The events of September 11 served as a wake-up call in many areas of government security, especially the INS. Immediately after it was clear that the nation was under attack, the government ordered the INS to tighten the borders, putting all inspectors on the highest state of alert. Air borders were essentially closed after President Bush ordered all planes en route to the United States diverted and all domestic flights canceled. Seaports remained open, as did entry points at the Canadian and Mexican borders.

Under the protocol for the high state of alert, border agents (INS as well as Customs officers, who inspected cargo crossing the border) were told to search people, their cars, and their luggage thoroughly—no matter how long each search took. Not surprisingly, the lines at border points were long and the waits at the entry points reached unheard-of lengths. Some travelers at the U.S.-Mexican border waited as long as twenty-one hours to get across.

One Wisconsin man recalls how closely his car and trailer were inspected as his wife and he returned from a vacation in Mexico. Not only did agents do a visual scan, but they used mirrors to inspect the undercarriage of the car and trailer, and even used dogs to sniff underneath the frame. "The guy ahead of me was body-searched, but I managed to avoid that," he says. "I did have to unload all of our coolers and suitcases, though—and that took forever."[7]

Others had similar experiences, but say that they were struck by how cooperative people were, even though the intensity of the searches made them very time-consuming. Wayne, a retired airline worker who was crossing the border from Canada, says that he was more than happy to endure delays if it would help keep terrorists out. "These [border] agents were doing their jobs, and they were being real careful," he says. "When they finished asking me the questions and looking around at my car, I told them, 'Thank you.' The last thing you want is more terrorists coming in."[8]

U.S. Customs officials conduct thorough vehicle searches at a border checkpoint in Washington State.

Trying to Be Thorough

But while many people were glad for the thoroughness at the border crossings, there was a downside for the border agents themselves. The round-the-clock high alert meant longer hours for INS and Customs agents. At one crossing point on the Mexican border, a supervisor was worried about his agents working extended hours in the one-hundred-plus-degree temperatures. "They are absolutely getting weary," he said. "The body can only take so much physically. The guys are working sixteen-hour shifts in heat that'll knock you down."[9]

The long shifts took a toll on the agents, and by October 2001 it was evident that they needed help. Although President Bush had promised a much larger budget for border control—especially for hiring more agents—it would take time to hire and train them. In the meantime, the National Guard was deployed to areas on the Canadian and Mexican borders to provide temporary assistance.

Some officials were concerned that the presence of armed soldiers at the borders would be alarming to people entering the United States. However, some of the soldiers involved felt that the reaction to their presence was very positive. Perhaps, they reasoned, people felt more secure knowing that the nation was serious about keeping terrorists out of the country, and the sight of a soldier in uniform reinforced that feeling.

A soldier in the National Guard inspects a vehicle at the Canadian border. The National Guard helps border inspectors during heightened security alerts.

Enormous Mismanagement

But while the temporary assistance of the National Guard helped ease the staffing problems at the border, the underlying problems were not solved. Within several months, it became apparent that the agency itself was not able to handle the responsibilities with which it was charged.

One of the last straws, for public and governmental critics alike, occurred six months after the attacks. In what appeared almost cruelly ironic, the INS sent the Florida flight school, where two of the hijackers had learned to fly airplanes, copies of visas for the two men to extend their visit to the United States as student pilots. To Americans, still reeling from the attacks, the mix-up was seen as inexcusable. Not only had the INS allowed terrorists into the United States to begin with, but the bureaucracy was so muddled that months after the two men had committed suicidal terrorist acts, the agency granted them an extension on their stay.

In Washington, D.C., politicians called for an end to the INS. One member of the House Judiciary Committee called the issuing of visas to the dead terrorists just another example of the mismanagement of the INS. "We've all been dumfounded by these revelations," he said.[10]

Senator Edward Kennedy agreed, insisting that the mistake was far from a simple mix-up, but proof that the INS had had no idea of the whereabouts or activities of the two hijackers. Kennedy blamed the INS for not installing a computer system which was supposed to track the movements of foreign students. "We cannot continue to tolerate a flawed information gathering and tracking system," he said, "that allows potential terrorists to enter or remain in the United States."[11]

Other Washington leaders were less critical of the agency. They believed that the INS was an easy target, and that Congress had to take some of the blame for the absence of an INS computer tracking network. After all, Congress had agreed to postpone the start of the new system when education groups complained that not only would tracking the movements of foreign students be invasive, but it would add a mountain of paperwork to colleges and universities. Many echoed earlier feelings—that the INS needed to be reformed, for it had too much responsibility. President Bush agreed, saying that Commissioner James Ziglar should be given a bit more time to fix the problems of the INS. "He's held accountable," said the president. "His responsibility is to reform the INS. Let's give him time to do so." [12]

A Variety of Complaints

The American public was just as divided in its assessment of the situation. Some agreed that the borders were too busy, but thought that perhaps the agents had not received training necessary to do the difficult job. "This is what people mean," grumbled one high school English teacher, "by government inefficiency." [13]

But while some criticized the INS for its lack of scrutiny of immigrants, others complained that the U.S. borders had become positively unfriendly since September 11—especially toward anyone of Middle Eastern descent. Especially indignant were U.S. citizens whose heritage was Middle Eastern; they often protested that they felt as though border agents were treating them with suspicion and, in some cases, with disdain. Some Americans were sympathetic to charges that immigrants were being treated with suspicion, but others insisted that the extra scrutiny of people who appeared to be Middle Eastern or Muslim was warranted. "I'm sorry people feel discriminated against," says one teacher, "but feelings are raw in the United States now. We have people who have sworn that we are the enemy, and they are Middle Eastern. How can we blame the border guards for being careful?" [14]

"It Worries Me"

Even though some critics charged that INS agents were being too careful, within six months of the terrorist attacks there

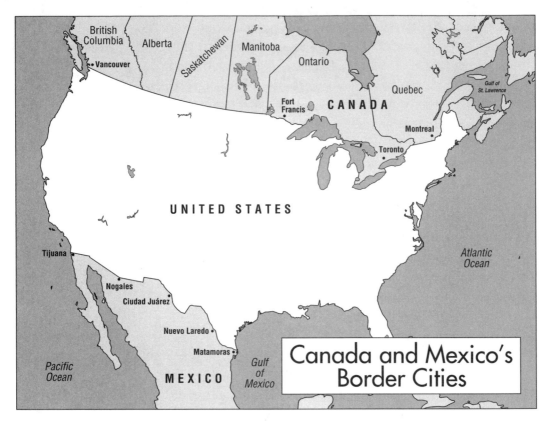

Canada and Mexico's Border Cities

was evidence that the thoroughness shown by border inspectors after September 11 was disappearing. Stories circulated about travelers being waved through border checkpoints with only a cursory inspection—or no inspection at all.

One Minnesota dentist of Middle Eastern descent returned to the United States from a fishing trip in Canada. Prepared for a lengthy interview and search at the border—in part because of his Pakistani name—he was astonished when U.S. agents simply waved him through the border. While the speedy crossing saved him time, he says, he was left with an uneasy feeling. "It worries me," he says. "It sounds odd, perhaps, but I don't mind the searches. I'm a citizen of the United States, and am as worried about terrorism as anyone else. I want them to be vigilant, to stop people that look like they might be from the part of the world that is currently on our 'bad guy' list."[15]

Government investigators, working undercover, found similar problems with border security late in 2002. Reporting to a Senate panel, one team of investigators said that they had experienced no difficulty entering the country using fictitious names together with fake documents, including invalid driver's licenses and counterfeit birth certificates. They had entered the United States from both Mexico and Canada, and told the panel that officials never once questioned the authenticity of the counterfeit documents they provided. What made the results of the investigation that much worse was that the documents were such poorly made forgeries. "Bouncers at college," noted Iowa senator Charles Grassley, "could spot the kind of fake IDs that were used by investigators."[16]

A New Department

The Senate investigation showed that the borders were as porous as they had been before September 11, and few leaders were

Senator Byron Dorgan calls for more stringent security measures at U.S. border crossings during a hearing on the security status of the Canadian borders.

23

willing to defend the status quo. Finally convinced that the INS was broken beyond repair, the administration proposed a new bureaucracy to Congress. All agencies that had had a presence at the border would be combined into one new agency called Customs and Border Protection, or CBP.

Officials announced that the new bureau would streamline border crossings. In the past, Customs inspectors were in charge of making sure that baggage or cargo was not dangerous. INS agents were supposed to make sure everyone crossing the border showed proper documentation. Still another agency, the Agricultural Plant Health and Inspection Service, watched for any illegal plants or food items being brought across the border. Under the new system, there would be fewer people asking questions about luggage, cargo, and passengers.

The bureau would have thirty thousand full-time employees—seventeen thousand inspectors and at least ten thousand agents patrolling the borders, watching for illegal crossings as well as securing the borders from possible terrorist activities, illegal weapons, or anything else that might compromise U.S. security. The CBP would be under the control of the new Department of Homeland Security, formed by President Bush shortly after September 11.

To handle the enforcement and investigation of immigration issues, another new agency, the Bureau of Immigration and Customs Enforcement, was created and was scheduled to begin its duties in March 2003. This agency would be made up of at least fourteen thousand employees, including fifty-five hundred criminal investigators and four thousand immigration and deportation agents. Agency officials were aware that keeping accurate records of the whereabouts of foreign visitors in the United States could very well prevent another terrorist attack.

Finally, to handle the old INS's immigration duties, another new agency called the Bureau of Citizenship and Immigration Services would focus on providing services for immigrants, such as processing work authorizations and

U.S. Customs officials check identification at the U.S.-Mexico border.

applications for U.S. citizenship, handling the administration of visas, and providing support for new residents and citizens. It, too, would be part of the Department of Homeland Security.

Officials of the new agencies insisted that the reorganization would enable them to do their various jobs more efficiently. However, officials conceded that fighting terrorism was definitely the priority behind the shuffling of the bureaucracy.

An Impossible Task?

But while the reorganization of the nation's border guards might have been a step in the right direction, many agents say that it will take more than that to secure the nation's borders. Some scoff that it can never be done. For example, agents along the Mexican border say they have been trying for years to stem the flow of illegal drugs and the smuggling of humans into the United States. They say there are simply too many crossing points to patrol.

Short of building a wall from the Pacific Ocean to the Gulf of Mexico, border agents say, there is no way to guarantee that a terrorist or a dangerous weapon cannot get past the border. With hundreds of thousands of vehicles and more than a million people crossing into the United States each day, searching every car and truck would mean impossible delays—and the odds of finding a poison or weapon that could be used by terrorists would still be slim.

There is no doubt that stopping illegal entry is extremely difficult, with thousands of miles of coastline, millions of people crossing the borders daily, and the enormous volume of cargo moving into the United States each day. However, the alternative—not catching the enemies at the border, before they can attack the United States again—is something that is too terrible to imagine. "We are taking on the protection of our borders . . . at a time of a real national threat to our security," says Border and Transportation Security undersecretary Asa Hutchinson, "but we are up to the task."[17]

Chapter Two

The Economic and Political Faces of the Border

Initially, when the border agencies were put on high alert after the attacks of September 11, there were few complaints. People—especially Americans—understood that the delays and searches at the nation's borders were necessary to prevent another act of terrorism. The inconvenience of long lines seemed a small price to pay for keeping terrorists out of the country.

Not a Small Price at All

But the delays were exacting a large price on many businesses in the United States who depend on quick, smooth border crossings each day to keep production going. American corporations depend on electrical and automotive components from all over the world. As one observer notes, "These days . . . a personal computer is a veritable global smorgasbord of chips, disks, and other gear, so the international supply pipeline provides the industry's lifeblood."[18]

Although American companies buy parts from companies worldwide, by far the greatest amount of their trade is with their closest neighbors, Mexico and Canada. Corporations like Samsonite, Levi Strauss, Sears, Memorex, and Caterpillar have operated small factories, called maquiladoras, in border areas of Mexico for decades, taking advantage of a ready supply of unskilled workers who work far more cheaply than

A truck driver waits at the U.S.-Mexican border while U.S. Customs agents inspect the contents of his truck. Border delays have proved costly for businesses.

American workers. The products turned out by the *maquiladoras* are crucial to those companies, and thousands of delivery trucks each day cross into the United States. All together, there is $250 billion a year in cross-border trade between Mexico and the United States.

Canadian businesses, too, are critical to American corporations. General Motors (GM) alone depends on six hundred truckloads of Canadian automotive parts each day to build its cars and trucks in Detroit. In recent years, many American factories have opted for what is known as "just-in-time" manufacturing, organizing shipments of parts to be delivered within hours of when they are needed. This has eliminated the need for costly warehouses to store components.

The just-in-time method works well, say many corporate executives, unless there are unexpected delays in delivery. "If you have hundreds of trucks waiting in line," says one GM spokesperson, "and you lose a minute on each truck, that adds up."[19]

Level One Alert

On September 11, companies in the United States, Mexico, and Canada saw what could happen when far more than a minute or two on each truck slowed border crossings. Border agents were put on a Level One alert, which meant that all persons and vehicles coming into the country could be searched and evaluated before being allowed to cross the border. While most of the crossings in Mexico and Canada remained open, bridge crossings, such as the Ambassador Bridge linking Detroit and Windsor, Ontario, closed completely.

More than 25 percent of all U.S. trade with Canada comes over the Ambassador Bridge, with six thousand trucks crossing into the United States each day. When it was closed, there was a line of trucks and cars extending more than twenty-five miles, waiting to cross into Michigan. Although the bridge was reopened shortly, the wait was about sixteen hours to get to the inspection booth, and once there, trucks and cars that before had been given only a cursory check were scrutinized thoroughly. Some drivers reported that their trucks were offloaded and searched—and that the process took between one and two hours.

The delays had a ripple effect on both sides of the border. U.S. plants awaiting late shipments were forced to shut down for days or weeks. Those closures affected some Canadian factories, which were forced to slow or stop production, or in some cases, lay off workers. Few disagreed that the attacks of September 11 had seriously endangered the $475 billion-per-year trading relationship between the two nations.

"The Economy Would Be Ruined"

Responding to the American public's nervousness about the possibility of further attacks, the Bush administration warned border agents to continue their precautions. However, business owners began to complain. Instead of being too lenient, the border agents were now accused of taking too much time in allowing people and vehicles to cross.

Many of the loudest critics were U.S. businesses in the Southwest, which depended heavily on Mexican workers. At the border crossing at San Ysidro, California, for example, fifty thousand Mexicans cross legally each day because they work in and around San Diego. Delays in processing the long lines of vehicles meant waiting an extra six to eight hours, and many of those workers were not able to get to their jobs on time.

Industries such as tourism, manufacturing, meat-packing, and the restaurant industry employ many Mexican workers, business owners said, and without them hundreds of businesses would crumble. Such businesses lobbied their representatives in Congress, and soon border agents were hearing a different message. One inspector understood that he and his fellow agents had to shorten their evaluations, that they "[could not] spend minutes inspecting vehicles, because the economy would be ruined."[20]

It was clear that there must be a balanced approach to the U.S. borders with Canada and Mexico. It is critical to have a system to secure national borders from terrorists and weapons of mass destruction. However, the system cannot be so slow that it damages the economy—either that of the United States or its neighbors.

Effects Across the Borders

Canadians and Mexicans did feel the economic effects of the terrorist attacks of September 11. After all, almost 90 percent of Mexican exports are destined for the United States. As a result, a number of Mexican businesses were devastated by the border slowdowns. The Mexican trucking industry, for example, lost more than $95 million in the months after the attacks, due, in part, to an economic slowdown that decreased demand for imports from Mexico.

Another important reason for financial loss was that, despite the slowdown, a larger number of trucks was needed simply to fill orders. The long waits at borders meant trucks that formerly could make several trips each day could only make one. To avoid being late in getting shipments to so many of their customers, the companies were forced to buy more trucks that could make local deliveries while their others were stuck in border lines. The cost of the extra vehicles was staggering to the trucking association.

In Canada, other businesses besides factories were affected by the slow border crossings. The Casino Windsor, in Windsor, Ontario, which boasts a twenty-three–story hotel as well as a variety of gambling venues, had enjoyed great success since it opened in 1993. More than 80 percent of its customers were Americans, who casino officials say seemed to enjoy gambling in a foreign country for a few hours. Thirteen thousand people each day crossed over the Ambassador Bridge to visit the Casino Windsor.

President Bush inspects a truck with a U.S. Customs agent at a Texas border crossing. Increased U.S. security has hurt economic relations with Mexico and Canada.

The manager recalls how, after the attacks on September 11, there was a dramatic change in the casino. "It hit us that afternoon," he says. "As [the huge crowd of Americans] left to go home, there was no one coming in."[21] Casino owners assumed the slowdown would last only a week or so, but learned that the slow border crossings would deter many of their American customers from returning. Within a month, Casino Windsor's business was down an alarming 70 percent, and the establishment was forced to lay off six hundred of its forty-eight hundred employees.

A few casinos opened on the U.S. side of the bridge, taking over much of the Windsor's clientele. Americans acknowledged that the Detroit casinos were not as elegant or nearly as large, but they were glad not to have to spend hours waiting in lines. Ironically, by November the waits had shrunk significantly—down to twenty minutes—but rumors of two- to three-hour waits persisted, preventing the casino from rebounding.

Border Politics

President Bush and his administration were aware after September 11 that to be successful in keeping tight, secure borders, the United States would have to have help from its neighbors. Because of the economic woes Mexico and Canada felt after the attacks, it seemed obvious that those nations would be happy to cooperate. However, U.S. officials soon learned that there were political issues that initially got in the way of such cooperation.

The sudden need for tighter borders by its northern neighbor was discouraging to Mexico. Prior to September 11, Mexican president Vicente Fox and George W. Bush had both proclaimed the beginning of a new era of trust and cooperation between their countries. President Bush made a visit to Mexico City his first international trip after his inauguration. And on September 6, 2001, President Fox visited the United States and addressed Congress.

Fox had hoped for more lenient borders with the United States. Unemployment and a worsening economy were prompting an increase in the number of Mexicans who wanted to work in the United States, and the Mexican president hoped that they would be allowed to enter legally. There seemed a strong possibility that the leaders could work something out—until disaster struck five days later.

Changing Priorities

Understandably, there was a rapid switch in priorities on September 11. No longer focused on immigration reform, President Bush called for even tighter control of the borders. Many Mexicans were affected by the slower border crossings and, instead of sympathizing with the United States, blamed America for what they viewed as punishing Mexico for the terrorist attacks. They were strongly opposed to getting involved in what they perceived was America's war on terrorism. In a poll taken several weeks after the attacks, 62 percent of Mexicans wanted their president to keep their country neutral. It seemed that the good start the two presidents had made before September 11 had all but disappeared.

Tony Garza, the new U.S. ambassador to Mexico, explained how much the United States needed Mexican cooperation at that time. In a speech to an assembly of Mexican college students he said, "There's an old Spanish proverb: 'In good times, all your friends know who you are. In bad times, you know who your friends are.' We often talk about the special relationship between our countries. The real test of that is stepping forward for each other in difficult times."[22]

But the prevailing view in Mexico was less than supportive at first, and leaders in Washington were impatient. Some members of Congress proposed retaliating economically by deporting tens of thousands of undocumented migrant workers in the United States, or by closing off the border indefinitely—an act that could severely damage Mexico's economy.

"It's a New Mission"

In March 2003, President Fox agreed to offer help to the United States. Even though some Mexican voters have remained unsupportive of the United States, Fox understood that they would be even less supportive if the border were closed because of the lack of cooperation.

One important bit of assistance was the addition of eighteen thousand Mexican soldiers to the U.S. side of the border. At present, some help at airports, seaports, and bridges that link Mexico and the United States, and half of the troops act as sentries in the desert that makes up much of the shared border. One sentry in Juárez noted the irony of the situation. "It's a new mission: Mexico looking out for the United States."[23]

Another cooperative effort involves the sharing of information between American and Mexican intelligence agencies. One official of Cisen, the Mexican version of the CIA,

A Mexican soldier stands guard at the Texas border. After the September 11 attacks, Mexico sent eighteen thousand soldiers to help the United States defend its borders.

says that their mission is fairly straightforward: to make sure that smugglers—whether dealing in drugs or weapons—are apprehended before they can cross the border from Mexico into the United States. "Mexico is not going to be used as a transit point," he vows, "for any terrorist or anyone who wishes to harm the United States."[24]

Politics in the North

Mexico was not the only neighbor who had reservations about offering support to the United States. While Canada's government was one of the first to express its sympathy after the attacks, some Canadians became upset over the economic effect the slow borders had on their economy. There was another issue, too. For years Canadians have been concerned that their importance is dwarfed by their neighbor to the south—that they are, as one Canadian official quips, "just a garage built onto the back of the American mansion."[25]

However, John Manley, the foreign affairs minister of Canada, was eager to work with the United States on beefing up border security on both sides. "We feel that we were equally under attack," he noted, insisting that his nation's concerns about being overshadowed by the United States needed to take a backseat to security. "There are no borders when terrorism strikes. If we weren't committed to our best friend and ally, just what would we be committed to?"[26]

Manley agreed with U.S. officials that a dramatic overhaul of the border was necessary. The Canadian government appropriated $443 million toward that end—much of it to add computers and border guards. In addition, Canadian intelligence combined with the FBI and CIA to create what is called a North American "zone of confidence." That meant the two nations would share databases about immigration, airline passenger lists, and other intelligence matters.

When asked about Canadians' nervousness about losing sovereignty, Manley explained that it was important for them to be realistic. He said he had assured President Bush that he

wanted the Canadian people to understand that they benefit best when they have a good relationship with the United
States. And after September 11, the best way to cement that
relationship would be by sharing the responsibility of their
common borders.

"We've got one customer who buys 87 percent of our
products," he said, "and if they think there's a problem with
security, there's a problem with security. That's not a con-
cession of sovereignty; that's just knowing the customer has
a concern, and therefore it's our concern."[27]

Preventing the Unimaginable

Improving economic and political associations with Canada
and Mexico, however, requires effective, secure borders. Even
with the cooperation of its neighbors, the United States
knows that the ultimate responsibility for maintaining its
borders lies with the men and women of the Customs and
Border Protection agency. They acknowledge that the pressure is intense. If they are to keep the borders moving swift-
ly enough for business, they have to make smart decisions
in a very short time.

"Inspectors typically have 25 to 30 seconds to make a
judgment about whether a driver is telling the truth," explains
one inspector on the Canadian border. "A lot of what we do
is just common sense. It's looking for things that are out of
place, a story that doesn't make sense, or if [a driver] is eva-
sive or won't look you right in the eye."[28]

It is not only the people they must observe, but also the
cargo being transported. Thousands of trucks pass through
each inspection station each day, with a wide range of cargo—
everything from automotive components and semiconduc-
tors to lumber, livestock, and steel. The hiding places for a
weapon that can be used for an act of terrorism are endless.

That is why, inspectors say, they cannot let their minds
wander at all; everyone at the border must remember that
even one lapse can mean that a concealed weapon slips across

U.S. homeland security adviser Tom Ridge (left) poses with Canadian foreign affairs minister John Manley after signing a new security agreement between the two nations in 2002.

the border. One agent who works on the Ambassador Bridge connecting Windsor to Detroit says that his coworkers are confident in their abilities. "We don't even talk about what happens if something gets through," he says. "Every day, we say we're going out there and stop[ping] *everything*."[29]

Help from Technology

One method that has helped the inspectors at the Ambassador Bridge near Detroit be both thorough and quick is a new paperless reporting system called the National Customs Automation Program, or NCAP. Using NCAP, information about what a truck's cargo is, as well as data on its driver, is transmitted from Canada to the United States in advance of the truck's arrival at the border. When a driver gets to the inspection booth, a bar-coded document is handed over to be scanned. As long as everything matches the computer information, the driver is allowed to proceed.

Up to six thousand big trucks cross the Ambassador Bridge from Canada into Detroit each day. Technology has helped speed up the inspection process.

Trucks that use NCAP are the big haulers for the Detroit automakers or other large U.S. corporations. Since about four thousand of the six thousand trucks that cross the bridge each day from Canada are big haulers, this saves a tremendous amount of time for the inspectors at the bridge. Before this system was used, a truck might take more than an hour to clear customs—especially if its paperwork was incomplete. Now a truck can be processed in a matter of a few seconds.

Experts say that the system may be even faster in the future. At least one automaker in Detroit is experimenting with truck-mounted transmitters, which would beam the barcodes and other data to the inspectors at the border when the truck is still on the bridge. If that system works, trucks may get the go-ahead to drive in a special lane that bypasses the border checkpoint entirely.

Looking for Dirty Bombs

There are other ways border agents can keep cargo searches brief—especially when looking for what is known as a dirty bomb. A dirty bomb is a conventional explosive device, made from dynamite, for example, but packed with radioactive material. The bomb would not only cause death and injury from the actual explosion, but would cause illness from the contamination of airborne radiation. Border agents are well aware of the dangers of such devices; in fact, most agree that a dirty bomb is their biggest concern.

To help them detect the presence of any radioactive materials in cargo, inspectors at both the Mexican and Canadian borders wear radiation detectors. At the Blue Water Bridge

A dirty bomb explodes in front of an overturned bus during a 2003 bioterrorism drill in Seattle. Border agents are especially vigilant against smugglers of these radioactive explosives.

between Port Huron Michigan and Sarina, Ontario, inspectors even check 150 garbage trucks each day. The trucks bring garbage from Ontario to landfills near Detroit, and some experts have noted that terrorists might try to smuggle a dirty bomb that way—perhaps believing the agents would not spend time on trucks carrying waste.

While the detecting devices are a key part of the agents' equipment, they have been found to be too sensitive by many inspectors. Agents complain that they go off whenever radioactive material is present—even in a small degree. That means cancer patients who have undergone radiation will trigger the alarm, as will those who have had radiation treatment for a thyroid condition and people who have been injected with radioactive fluid for certain heart scans. When that happens, agents must wave the traveler aside and give the vehicle a careful search—which can take hours.

Border agents are apologetic, and they realize the detectors have caused many travelers to become angry. One fifty-two-year-old engineer with a thyroid condition was stopped eight times within a four-month period. He says he is tired of being looked at with suspicion. "I'd be glad to get a notarized letter from my doctor or something. Anything to avoid being treated like I'm smuggling a dirty bomb in my shirt or something."[30]

U.S. Border Patrol officers stand guard at a bridge in Buffalo, New York. Bridges and other vulnerable targets are carefully patrolled when the national security alert is heightened.

Optimism Amid Challenges

Border agents feel that they have made great strides since September 11. For example, when the war on terrorism expanded to Iraq early in 2003, many worried that the border situation might resemble the chaos of September 11—but they were pleasantly surprised. Although on the first day of the war, lines were longer than normal at both borders, the waits were nothing like they had been in 2001.

One Toronto auto parts manufacturer attributes the improvement to the border staff. "We now have a much better trained staff," he says. "They can process people and goods much better than they could before."[31] The agents themselves agree. They say that they take their jobs very seriously and feel confident that they are doing the best they can, and every day brings the promise of improved methods and new technology that will make them even better and quicker.

But while there has been progress, some feel that the nation is not moving fast enough in securing its borders. Not every vehicle is searched, and there is concern that even with the billions of dollars allocated for border security, Americans are fooling themselves if they think the borders are impenetrable. Representative Jim Ramstad of Minnesota believes that there is much left to be done. "Our nation's border security is our homeland's Achilles' heel," he says. "I think border *insecurity* is a more honest and accurate term. Our borders are porous."[32]

Border officials acknowledge that there are still improvements to be made, and they are convinced that they are up to the task. "This is an historic opportunity for all of us," says one senior official of the CBP, "and despite tremendous resistance within government to change, we've got new priorities and new concerns. There are ways to reorganize to bring efficiency and effectiveness to our country's border security, and I'm confident we're going to do it."[33]

Chapter Three

The Human Borders

Plans to strengthen the nation's borders have had to balance economic considerations. However, the attempts to apply more muscle to its border security have affected more than dollars and cents. They have caused changes in the way border communities live, how criminals break the law, and especially how the residents of Canada and Mexico view the United States as a neighbor.

"It's Absurd, and It's Offensive"

The tightening of the U.S.-Canadian border, for instance, has brought a storm of protest from individuals for whom crossing back and forth is a daily occurrence. Many people do not realize how close together some Canadian and American communities are. In fact, there are some towns that actually lie across the border—half in Canada, half in the United States. There are even golf courses where a tee may be in one nation, while the green is in another.

In some of these northern communities the border is unmanned, and residents have a long history of crossing—often several times each day—to shop, to visit friends, or to work. In cases where a road does have a formal border, agents merely waved them through, smiling at familiar faces. However, some aspects of the border changed dramatically on September 11.

Traffic backs up at an Ontario border crossing as a result of stricter security measures. Tightening a once-open border has caused some friction between the two nations.

U.S. border officials were instructed to demand documentation from any Canadian who wanted to enter the country, no matter how familiar his or her face. Suggests one U.S. border spokesperson, "It's probably wise to bring as much documentation as you can—a passport, or if you don't have that, a birth certificate, to make things easier on everybody."[34]

But while Canadians were sympathetic about the terrorist attacks of September 11, many were furious about what they perceived as a sudden hostility. One Ontario woman crosses the border several times a week to shop and visit with friends, and says she feels a coldness in how she is treated. "I'll tell you what it's like," she says angrily. "It's like I've been shopping in my corner market for thirty years or more, and I know the people who own it and suddenly I pop in to buy milk or cigarettes or something. And guess what? They don't seem to know me anymore, and demand to see identification before I am permitted to write a check. It's absurd, and it's offensive."[35]

Fifty Feet

The problem was pushed into the international spotlight in October 2002, when Michel Jalbert, a thirty-two-year-old forestry worker from the village of Pohenegamook, Quebec, was arrested when he drove his truck to Oullete's, a gas station only fifty feet inside the U.S. border. Oullete's is in Estcourt Station, Maine, a community of four people. (Since September 11, villagers who cross from Pohenegamook into Estcourt Station are supposed to report their comings and goings to the U.S. border outpost three-quarters of a mile away.) While to many the ritual of registering seems pointless, border agents have been instructed to make certain they check *all* who enter and exit the country.

But residents said that almost everyone from Pohenegamook buys gas at Oullete's—after all, the gas is often as much as twenty cents per gallon cheaper than Canadian gas. They also point out that the gas station is on a little spit of land surrounded by dense forest, reachable only from a driveway that starts in Quebec and ends in Maine. "There's not even a fence there," protests Jalbert. "It was an invisible line. And crossing it was a habit."[36]

Jalbert was sentenced to five weeks in jail for his border violation, but U.S. secretary of state Colin Powell intervened to try to smooth ruffled feathers. Powell acknowledged the openness between the two communities. However, he warned that the laxness of border rules could be exploited by some people. "We know that there are terrorists out there who will try to use that openness [between Canada and the United States] to attack either one of our two countries."[37]

While Powell's comments did appease some Canadians, some felt that there was a new atmosphere of heavy-handedness by U.S. officers at the Canadian border. The *Montreal Gazette* condemned the actions of U.S. agents working at the border, saying that such "small-time mean-spiritedness sends a louder message to Canadians than Powell's vague assurance. Powell might be sensitive to the damage done to U.S.-Canada relations, but the U.S. officials on the ground, it's painfully obvious, are not."[38]

The Most Porous Border

The United States has maintained that while Canadian officials have been cooperative to speed up border crossings for economic reasons, they have not done enough to keep their own borders secure from terrorists. As many as fifty foreign terrorist organizations are known to be currently operating in Canada—all of them targeting the United States. And that, say U.S. officials, is because of the laxness of Canada's borders.

While none of the nineteen hijackers of September 11 entered the United States from Canada, at least one known terrorist was arrested after leaving Canada for Port Townsend, Washington. Ahmed Ressam, who in 1999 was on his way to

Oullette's gas station (background) in Maine was popular with Canadian drivers. Access to the station became difficult, however, with the post-9/11 security measures.

blow up Los Angeles International Airport, had been admitted into Canada even though he had been accused of terrorism in Algeria.

"Canadians like to have a more open border with us," says one northern Minnesota resident, "because that benefits them. But they're not the ones being threatened by all these terrorist groups—we are. And if they want an open border between us, they have to be more vigilant about keeping these extremists out of Canada in the first place."[39]

James Bissett, a retired Canadian ambassador, agrees. He says that it is has been far too easy for people to enter Canada, and the United States is quite correct in being nervous. "We sell our citizenship very cheaply," he says. "We have admitted 37,000 refugee claimants since September 11, five or six thousand from the Middle East. About 60 percent of them are smuggled in by international criminal gangs, and we don't know who . . . these people are. We aren't controlling our borders, and we won't until something catastrophic happens or until the Americans order us to do something."[40]

"Every Single Stop, Every Single Airport"

Because the United States was not satisfied that Canada was strict enough with its own borders, U.S. border agents have been more thorough in their questioning of some Canadians crossing the borders, in particular those who are of Middle Eastern descent and/or are Muslim.

In one highly publicized case, a Syrian-born Canadian citizen who was on his way home to Montreal from Tunisia landed at New York's John F. Kennedy International Airport. He was only transferring flights, but U.S. officials detained him. Believing the man to have ties with al-Qaeda, they deported him to Syria without consulting with the Canadian government.

Many Canadians were angry, and accused the United States of being overreactive and racist. "Canadian citizens have a right to be treated as Canadian citizens," protested one

Canadian official, "wherever they were born."[41] Others add that American scrutiny of Muslims and Middle Eastern people is a serious human rights issue that needs to be addressed.

Some in the United States agree with the Canadians. They, too, feel that using race or religion to determine who gets scrutinized by border agents is unfair and a violation of civil rights. Others, however, say that since the hijackers of September 11 were all Middle Eastern Muslim men, it makes sense to look at that segment of the traveling public more carefully. "Who should we be asking [border officials] to take a look at?" asks one airline worker. "Should we have them concentrate on little old grandmas? Isn't it common sense to look at Arabs and Muslims? You can bet if the situation were reversed, and Americans attacked a Middle Eastern country, they'd be looking carefully at any Americans."[42]

But Canadian officials are unconvinced. They see the American system of profiling as being an offense to some of their citizens, and they want it stopped. "We obviously cannot control what Americans do," says the director of Canada's Refugee Council, "but we must stand up to them. This profiling is proof that the United States is not a safe . . . country for refugees. . . . It is laughable to suggest that we are a threat to the United States."[43]

Rohinton Mistry, a Canadian author born in India, agrees. He canceled an American book tour after being stopped for random checks at airports in New York, Minneapolis, and Washington, D.C. "I don't find this is the random check that they talk about," he insists, "not when they happen to have it at every single stop, every single airport."[44]

"Cold, Hard Reality"

U.S. officials, however, are unwilling to tread more lightly in such matters. They admit that the status of their borders—especially the unmanned parts of the Canadian border—leave them with little choice but to be reactive when faced with a

Middle Easterner at the border. As a spokesperson for Washington's Center for Immigration Studies says,

> The cold, hard reality is that the U.S. has no control over its borders—7,000 miles of land borders alone—and is now very much in a reactive position. . . .We are in a war where borders are the front lines. . . . A war is being waged here by an army of foreign nationals. They are taking advantage of America's remarkable generosity, and their goal is mass murder. [Canada's] intelligence service has said that there are no fewer than 50 terrorist organizations operating in Canada. [Canada's] remarkably generous asylum policy [toward refugees] puts the U.S. in a uniquely vulnerable position.[45]

A Flood of Illegal Immigrants

The question of racial profiling is not as much of an issue along the Mexican border. Since September 11, border agents have been establishing more of a presence at the border as a whole, not only the crossing points. The goal is not only to keep terrorists out, but also to cut down on the drugs and people being smuggled across—a longstanding problem, especially along the Mexican border.

Of Mexico's 100 million people, between 45 and 50 million are living at or below the poverty level. Each year there are about three hundred thousand Mexicans who illegally cross into the United States, seeking opportunities they cannot find at home. Most come because Mexico's economy is in shambles, with unemployment at record highs. In fact, since September 11, another sixty thousand unskilled Mexican workers immediately joined the ranks of the unemployed—migrant workers in the United States who were sent home after the attacks.

The United States is an attractive idea, for there are always jobs—especially for unskilled workers. The United States does allow people to immigrate legally, but those selected are

A Mexican family waits for nightfall to cross illegally into the United States. Despite a two-thousand-mile-long border, illegal Mexican immigrants have difficulty evading U.S. border security.

usually only people with exceptional skills in some area. Too, those wishing legal immigration status must go through a process that may take many months, and even then there is no guarantee that they will be selected.

"You Would Think It Would Be Easy"

The only other option is finding some way to cross the border without being caught by the agents who patrol the area. "You would think it would be easy," says one young woman who crossed as a teenager in 1993. "You see that the border between our countries is almost two thousand miles, and you say that there's no way that *la migra* [Border Patrol] can guard it all. But it is very hard."[46]

Many echo her sentiment, saying that it is very common for people to try three or four times—or sometimes more—before they are successful. Ana was fourteen when she crossed into the United States from Tijuana, Mexico.

We had to wade in shallow water, walking almost two hours in the dark. . . . Otherwise, we would be faced with metal barricades on the land you can't get through. The first time the Border Patrol heard us, and we ran back [to the Mexican border] and we tried three days later. But then there were fireworks going on near the shore—some fiesta, I think. And we worried that we would be seen, with all the lights, so we went back then, too. I was so glad that we were successful the third time—we were feeling very unlucky.[47]

Coyotes

After September 11 millions of dollars were spent hiring more border agents for the U.S.-Mexican border. Although their primary mission was to catch terrorists entering the country illegally, agents have also caught more immigrants seeking a new life in the United States. Agents were provided with more technology, such as X-ray scanners that can show whether a

A semi trailer truck from Mexico undergoes X-ray inspection for illegal human cargo at the Texas border. New high-tech security systems have reduced illegal entries.

truck is carrying human cargo. Along the more remote borders, more walls, motion sensors, and cameras were installed. That made it even more difficult for people wanting to cross illegally.

The improvements in border security have affected the way people are attempting to illegally enter the United States. First, fewer people feel comfortable crossing without the help of a "coyote" or human smuggler. "Since 9/11," says the head of border security at Del Rio, Texas, "we have seen a massive increase in the numbers of people paying to be smuggled into the United States."[48] Before the security was stepped up, many people were willing to rely on their own wits to cross, even if it took several attempts.

The benefit of hiring a coyote is that a professional knows the best routes, and is able to provide illegal immigrants with fake Social Security cards or other documents once they arrive. In addition, coyotes have networks of people in border towns on the U.S. side that will help the immigrants get to their destination safely, without being apprehended by agents. "It's not like you're free once you get across [the border]," says one boy. "As long as you have no papers, nothing that proves you're legal, you can be arrested anytime. You just want to get to where you know you'll be safe, like if you have relatives already [in the United States]."[49]

Hiring a coyote has always been expensive, but since September 11 the price has skyrocketed. One twenty-two-year-old who asked not to be identified says that coyotes are getting thousands of dollars to bring one person across in 2003. He explains,

> Four years ago, my brother in Chicago sent home money for a coyote to bring our little sister here—$900! She was only thirteen then, and she could not have made it safely on her own [from southern Mexico]. It seemed very expensive at the time—my brother had to work a long time to earn that much. I came on my own when I was sixteen, and I have been back twice to

Mexico. Now I want to bring my girlfriend up, but the coyote—the same man my brother used before—is very expensive, almost $5,000.[50]

More Dangerous

However, the increase in smugglers' fees has not necessarily meant safer passage across the border. The coyotes have steered their clients away from the busy city borders where there is more security and threat of detection. Instead, many have routed their clients toward more desolate desert areas with fewer border agents. Unfortunately, the new routes have had tragic results for many of the immigrants.

When nineteen-year-old Yolanda set out with her ten-month-old daughter to join her husband in the United States, she hired a coyote. He put Yolanda and her baby in a group with nine others, and gave them instructions to walk to the Arizona border—a walk which would, he said, take them about six hours. However, the group wandered for four days in temperatures of 109 degrees, their water supply long since used up. Yolanda collapsed and died; but, although her baby was badly sunburned and dehydrated, she survived—only because Yolanda had given all the water to her.

Many experts feel that the large fees that coyotes can command since September 11 have brought many into the human smuggling business who are less careful about their clients' safety. Deaths such as Yolanda's have become all too common in recent months. For example, between January and September 2002, there were 141 deaths in the Arizona desert alone. Officials say that the figure reflects only the reported deaths; there have been at least that many unidentified bodies buried in paupers' graves, as well. The number might be higher yet without the efforts of the Border Patrol's elite search and rescue team members, who have saved almost six thousand illegal immigrants over the past three years.

Border agents feel that the coyotes are responsible for most of the deaths they see among illegal immigrants. "These smugglers couldn't care less about human life," says one agent. "It's become big business. The smuggling of human cargo now rivals that of drug smuggling."[51]

"Listening to Us, Watching Us"

Much of the drug traffic destined for the United States goes through Mexico—from marijuana grown there to heroin or cocaine that has come north from Colombia. Just as the tighter borders have created more risky routes for illegal immigrants, they have necessitated that drug traffickers become more creative in their smuggling as well.

According to experts, the flow of heroin, cocaine, and marijuana seemed to slow for a few weeks after the attacks of September 11. Smugglers were nervous, and waited until they could assess the new security procedures. One inspector says

A Mexican police officer monitors the entrance of a smuggling tunnel in a Mexican house. Such tunnels are mainly used for drug trafficking.

that they were under constant surveillance from hundreds of the unseen eyes and ears of smugglers "on both sides of the border, listening to us, watching us."[52]

When the trafficking started up in October, agents say that, because of the heightened security, they were seizing far more drugs than they ever had. While they have yet to apprehend a terrorist crossing the border, they have set records every month since the attacks for the amount of drugs seized. "We are real cognizant of the fact we have to keep that weapon of mass destruction from coming in," says one inspector. "That's everybody's greatest fear. But we're real proud of the fact that we're seizing so many drugs. It has been our anti-terrorism dividend."[53]

A Violent Alternative

Just as the more careful border searches since September 11 have changed the way coyotes smuggle illegal immigrants across the border, drug smugglers have changed tactics, too. At one time drugs were smuggled across the border in backpacks and secret compartments in cars—often by ordinary citizens who were paid for their trouble. Since September 11, however, drug traffickers themselves are often going to more remote, unmanned border crossings, and are moving millions of dollars' worth of their product at a time.

Using off-road vehicles and bodyguards armed with automatic weapons, traffickers often cross the border on private property or land owned by the U.S. National Park System. Organ Pipe Cactus National Monument, a park in southern Arizona, is widely regarded as the most dangerous park in the United States, for it is used almost daily by smugglers. Since 1998, three rangers at the park have been killed as they tried to arrest traffickers.

Park officials are angry, for they say rangers are not trained to do such police work. They feel that there should be more control by CBP or other government agencies at the parks. "We have caught people from China, Pakistan, and Yemen

Two Arizona civilians scan the Mexican border for illegal immigrants. Some citizens resort to such vigilante activity because they feel existing security measures are inadequate.

coming through," says one park ranger. "If one thousand illegal immigrants can walk through the desert here, so can one thousand terrorists."[54]

Vigilantes

The drug traffickers' tactics at the borders have had other consequences. Armed citizens' groups, some using high-tech scanners and satellite equipment, have begun patrolling the border areas. Although many have accused such groups of being no more than vigilantes, one citizens' group member disagrees. He says that they are only patrolling the borders because the federal government has not provided enough government agents to do the job. "We are answering the president's call to be vigilant," he maintains. "We are going to do the job that he refuses to do. He is not protecting American citizens. So we say either recruit us, train us, and support us—or stay the hell out of the way."[55]

Other residents see the citizens' patrols as having the potential to do far more harm than good. "I can see being angry about drug runners making roads through your property," says Earle, who lives in another remote border area in southern California. "If they can arrest these smugglers, do something about the easy access they have into the United States, I'm for it. But these ranchers chasing around in the desert with their night goggles and shotguns, running people down—that's crazy. It sounds more like the [Ku Klux] Klan to me."[56]

He believes that it is important for the United States to address the issues of smuggling and illegal immigration and how they relate to border security, and the sooner the better. "It sounds like our country better figure out a way to strike a balance here between human values and keeping terrorists out of here," he warns, "or we're going to be reading about one of these groups killing somebody—maybe a Mexican family just trying to get into the United States to have a better life. That's not what we want to do—I mean, that's not how America is supposed to work."[57]

Chapter Four

Securing America's Sea Borders

Securing about seventy-five hundred miles of land borders with Mexico and Canada is a difficult job, but those entrusted with protecting the ninety-five thousand miles of sea borders of the United States are faced with an almost impossible one. Long before the attacks of September 11, experts were warning that port security was the most glaring weakness in the nation's security network. In August 2000, a presidential advisory commission concluded that "the state of security in U.S. seaports generally ranges from poor to fair, and in a few cases good."[58]

The nation's 360 ports and extensive coastline got little attention, however, until after the terrorist attacks—and even then, making air traffic safer was the government's main priority. But many experts say that as flimsy as airline security was before September 11, port security was far worse. "If you think the aviation community is bad," says one transportation official, "the maritime community has never thought about security other than anti-piracy."[59]

A Host of Targets

For terrorists, seaports present a host of targets, simply because by their nature ports must be connected to cities and transportation. A dirty bomb detonated in a U.S. seaport, for instance, would affect far more than the port itself. Fourteen of the twenty largest American cities are on seaports, and nearby there are fuel terminals, nuclear power plants, and an infrastructure of highways, bridges, and railroads.

Stephen Flynn, a retired commander of the U.S. Coast Guard and senior fellow at the Council on Foreign Relations cites Newark, New Jersey, as an example. "In one mile," he explains, "you have one of the largest container ports in the world, you have the rail link that connects the northeast to the rest of the nation, you have the New Jersey turnpike and Newark International Airport."[60]

The ports are vital to the nation's economy—much more so than either air or land traffic. Approximately 95 percent of all U.S. foreign trade comes through seaports, and $1 trillion of the gross national product. According to Coast Guard admiral Terry Cross, "We think shutting down one or two major ports would do more damage to our economy than September 11."[61]

Park rangers guard the USS *Constitution* (background) after the national security alert is heightened. Tourist attractions are possible terrorist targets.

"Nuke in the Box"

The potential for sabotage of cargo containers frightens many experts the most. No fewer than 7.2 million huge metal cargo containers—the size of the trailer of a semi—arrive in U.S. ports each year. At the time of the terrorist attacks, most containers were assumed to contain whatever was marked on the ship's manifest—whether it was computer parts, furniture, electronic equipment, or any one of an endless list of goods imported each day. Even by September 2002, inspectors were only able to check 2 percent of the sixteen thousand containers that had arrived in U.S. ports every day of the year.

Inspectors worry about what they call the "nuke in the box" scenario, in which some sort of nuclear device is smuggled inside a container. As the National Academy of Sciences points out, there is a great amount of nuclear material circulating around the world, much of it stolen from the former Soviet Union. In an August 2002 report the organization noted, "Clandestine production of special nuclear material by states or terrorist groups . . . for use against the United States represents a significant and near-term threat to homeland security."[62]

Not only could containers be used to smuggle a weapon of mass destruction into the United States, they could be used to smuggle in terrorists themselves. In May 2002, a security report found that at least twenty-five extremists from the Middle East had likely infiltrated the U.S. border by stowing away in containers. In October 2002, Italian authorities found an al-Qaeda operative locked in a shipping container bound for Canada. Inside the container, the man had a bed, a makeshift bathroom, airport maps and security passes, and a phony airport mechanic's certificate.

However, the cargo containers on incoming ships are not the only danger. The ships themselves can be used as weapons, in much the same way airplanes were used on September 11. Cargo ships are very slow, but they are massive, and if a terrorist gained control of a ship and rammed a bridge, an oil

tanker, or an offshore nuclear power plant or petrochemical complex, it would be catastrophic.

The Coast Guard

The Coast Guard has always been responsible for keeping the nation's sea borders secure. However, before September 11, only 2 percent of the resources allotted the Coast Guard went toward securing ports and U.S. waters. Instead, most of its time and effort was spent enforcing the law that prohibits foreign fishing boats within two hundred miles of the borders, catching drug smugglers, enforcing anti-pollution laws, and helping boaters in distress.

For years, say members of the Coast Guard, they have been the poor relation to the marines or the U.S. Navy, with neither the budget nor the respect of those military branches. The Coast Guard's fleet is the seventh largest navy in the

A U.S. Coast Guard security boat patrols a harbor as a cargo ship enters. The Coast Guard is now part of the Department of Homeland Security.

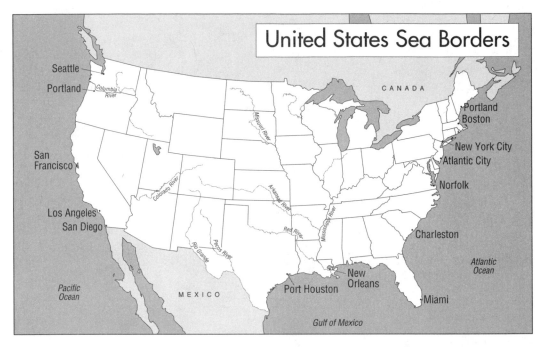

United States Sea Borders

Seattle
Portland
Columbia River
San Francisco
Los Angeles
San Diego
Pacific Ocean
Missouri River
Colorado River
Arkansas River
Red River
Mississippi River
Rio Grande
Pecos River
MEXICO
Port Houston
New Orleans
CANADA
Portland
Boston
New York City
Atlantic City
Norfolk
Charleston
Atlantic Ocean
Miami
Gulf of Mexico

world, but out of forty-one naval fleets in existence today, it ranks thirty-ninth in the age of its vessels. One reporter noted "leaky boats that are too often stuck at the pier, under repair; the gaps in its emergency communications network; [and] a self-perpetuating condition of short staffing and inexperience that demands constant overtime work."[63]

However, President Bush called for a 15 percent budget increase for the Coast Guard for 2003—the largest increase in U.S. Coast Guard history. In addition, the Coast Guard was added to the Department of Homeland Security, so it would have access to the same intelligence as the Customs and Border Protection agents.

Thinking Like Terrorists

In the months since September 11, the Coast Guard, together with other agencies in the Department of Homeland Security, has begun tackling the problems that could potentially be exploited by terrorists. Since the large volume of cargo containers is worrisome, that has been the first issue addressed in port security. One program utilizes U.S. inspectors in some of the largest seaports around the world, including Rotterdam, Singapore, and others from which much of U.S. cargo originates. By coordinating efforts with foreign inspectors, containers that may seem suspicious can be inspected carefully before they are even loaded on ships. By April 2003, the United States had signed agreements with eighteen ports worldwide.

Another important improvement in shipping is part of the Maritime Security Act, which President Bush signed in December 2002. Among other things, the act requires that any shipping company planning to arrive in a U.S. port must notify the Coast Guard within ninety-six hours before it arrives. In its notification, the shipping company must provide detailed information—where the ship originated, its crew list, a list of all its cargo, and its last port of call.

That information is relayed from the Coast Guard to the new National Vessel Movement Center in West Virginia.

A large volume of cargo is shipped to America from this marine terminal in Singapore. Singapore was the first port to agree to inspections of U.S.-bound shipments.

Investigators there check the specific data against intelligence and criminal databases. Knowing that a crew member may have been suspected of illegal activity, for example, may raise investigators' eyebrows, and can make the cargo a bit more suspect.

With early knowledge of cargo and crew, inspectors then go through the list of containers and give each a ranking for how much risk it entails, from 0 (no risk) to 300 (highest risk). Any container that gets a rank of 190 or more must be inspected by local agents before it arrives in a U.S. port. "If a container has some nasty stuff in it," explains one port official, "once it gets to this port, it's already too late. You want it to go back to the source."[64]

By the year 2010, the International Maritime Organization, an agency of the United Nations, will require all oceangoing commercial ships to have a transmitter that can broadcast such detailed information about its crew and cargo, as well as the ship's exact location and speed, as it is en route. In the United States that will save the Coast Guard time, because the West Virginia investigators will get the information directly—the moment the ship leaves port. Any ship that does not comply will become an immediate high-interest target for U.S. intelligence and the Coast Guard.

Boarders at the Borders

Another improvement that is helping the Coast Guard keep ports secure is the addition of special agents known as sea marshals. In the months following September 11, teams of sea marshals would intercept every ship that came within ten miles or so of the port.

As a ship approached port, armed teams of sea marshals would pull their boat alongside, board the ship, and monitor the crew as it was brought to port. Some headed to the engine room, some to the rear steering compartment, and some to the bridge of the vessel. All of these are places from which a terrorist could take over control of the ship.

Soon after the extra sea marshals were added, one ship captain said that he was glad to have the sea marshals around, for there were so many ways a terrorist could gain control of a ship. "A terrorist could infiltrate . . . the crew," he explained. "A terrorist could come on board a vessel on a stowaway kind of capacity—in a container, for example. A terrorist could board as a passenger."[65]

The increased presence of the sea marshals provided a sense of security; however, it became evident by September 2002 that the $1 million per day it cost to have them board each incoming ship was too much. Today, sea marshals still escort each ship, but they only board those that have raised some suspicion with the National Vessel Movement Center agents. Some are boarded if they have strayed from their course, or if the type of ship would be a tempting target for terrorists, such as a cruise ship, which carries up to five thousand civilians.

Sea marshals board a cruise ship in Alaska. Prohibitive costs prevent marshals from boarding all incoming ships.

One sea marshal says that if he is not comfortable with the feeling he gets while on the bridge with the crew, he

immediately assumes control. A typical order from a sea marshal in such circumstances, he says, would be, "All hands on the bridge are going to go ahead and get on their knees except for the essential personnel. We're going to lock down the bridge and provide security for the pilot."[66]

Checking the Cargo

Once a ship is in port, its cargo is again subjected to scrutiny. Although inspectors do not open most of the containers, those coming off any ship about which the Coast Guard has suspicions are all put through a system called the Vehicle and Cargo Inspection System, or VACIS. The system was developed in the late 1990s to help Customs inspectors search cargo for illegal drug shipments—especially along the Mexican border. However, after September 11 the government began purchasing VACIS units—at about $1 million apiece—in great numbers, using them all around the country to search for terrorist weapons.

Customs officers inspect cargo containers with an X-ray scanner in the Port of Los Angeles. Scanners are used to find illegal drugs and weapons.

The system used at the docks uses a long boom extending from the body of a truck. At the end of the boom is a box which shoots low-intensity gamma rays from a tiny pellet of a radioactive isotope. As the large cargo containers are rolled past the box, agents inside the truck view the image on a computer screen. Experts say that gamma rays are far more effective for this type of job than X rays, because gamma rays are not easily absorbed by solid material, and therefore can penetrate more than four inches of solid steel.

In March 2003, one reporter watched as a team of inspectors using the VACIS system looked at an image that appeared to be different than what it was labeled. "You see, this one is supposed to be household goods," said one inspector, "but look here." He pointed to a large cylindrical shape. "That's obviously something really dense, and it doesn't look like household goods," he said. "We're going to open that one up. Look, it could be a propane tank. It could be a statue." [67]

Whenever the VACIS image shows anything out of the ordinary, inspectors force open the container. In this case, the suspicious shape turned out to be an industrial oven which had been packed in the wrong crate, but agents know that they have no choice but to check each time there is any question. "It's the time you don't check something out, that's the time you'll wish you had," says one inspector. "Being careful sends a message to anyone who wishes the United States harm. It says there's a lot of people working here around the clock to protect our borders." [68]

Above the Water, Under the Water

In addition to trying to monitor the contents of the large number of cargo containers, the Coast Guard is applying a great deal of effort in other parts of port security. For instance, the Physical Oceanographic Real-Time System (PORTS) keeps track of data such as wind speed and direction, currents, and salt content of the water in a port area. Originally intended to give information to ship captains, this system of sensors and shore instruments was developed after a freighter that had no current information about port conditions rammed into a bridge in Tampa, Florida, killing thirty-five people.

Since September 11, experts have hoped that PORTS could be a valuable tool in fighting bioterrorism or ecoterrorism. If someone were to release toxins into the water, purposely causing an ecological disaster, PORTS would track the movement of such substances immediately, giving Coast Guard personnel enough of a warning so that they might be able to contain the problem. PORTS data about currents and wind can also tell Coast Guard officials which areas of a harbor are navigable at any given time. "It doesn't predict where a bad guy may pop up," says one San Francisco marine expert, "but it could predict—if someone's coming in a small boat—where they could or couldn't enter the bay and how."[69]

Most of the PORTS instruments are mounted on buoys, but the Coast Guard uses another tool that is kept completely underwater. Known as the UAV, short for Underwater Autonomous Vehicle, it looks like a small torpedo and can patrol a port area, gathering and transmitting several kinds of important data. UAVs can take samples of water to make certain it has not been poisoned, or take pictures of underwater bridge supports to make certain they have not been tampered with.

UAVs are very new, but already scientists are experimenting with a new generation of the instruments which will have even more capabilities, such as being able to stay underwater for very long periods of time. By docking every so often at underwater stations connected to shore by fiber-optic cables, the UAVs will be able to recharge their batteries, download information, and receive new instructions.

More Money Needed

But while a great deal of progress has been made in strengthening the security of the nation's sea borders, many officials insist that there is much more to be done. Senator Dianne Feinstein of California has been concerned that the ports are not getting money promised them after September 11. The federal government has been slow to provide the funds that have already been appropriated, she says, and as a result the ports are unable to purchase equipment and hire enough inspectors to do the job. "I believe," she says, "that our seaports remain almost as vulnerable today as they were before 9/11."[70]

Senator Fritz Hollins of South Carolina agrees. He has spoken angrily about Congress appropriating large amounts of money for border security, only to have lawmakers bicker about how it should be divided. By making border security a political issue and delaying the important funding, Hollins says, agencies are not getting funds when they need them. "Everybody talks about port security," he said disgustedly in April 2003, after Congress voted against releasing $1 billion for port security that had been appropriated earlier, "but they don't do anything about it. Every Republican and every Democrat committed to this funding . . . but they weren't willing to put the real dollars behind that commitment. They just aren't taking the issue seriously."[71]

It is not only lawmakers who are complaining. A high-ranking Coast Guard official was asked to give the president and the nation assurance that the nation's sea borders were being adequately defended. However, he declined. In his words, he was asked to say "that we've got a handle on this, that the maritime component of this national security package is okay. It is not. Do we have an adequate inventory of vessels, aircraft, and communications equipment? No, we do not."[72]

"The Answer Is Not Searching Every Container"

The lack of funds that actually reach the Coast Guard and the ports may be catastrophic, say some. Without the technology and the manpower necessary, the sea borders are in danger of being compromised. Trade experts predict a heavier volume of shipping trade—as much as double by 2020. With more than 14 million cargo containers coming to America's ports then, a well-organized system of security will be critical.

Even with the delays in funding, some are optimistic about the future of U.S. ports. Many who work in security say that since September 11 there has been a great deal more cooperation between the various intelligence-gathering agencies and the Coast Guard and Customs inspectors. Cooperation like that is even more critical at the international level—otherwise the task becomes overwhelming. "The answer," says one Coast Guard official, "is not searching every container. I think the answer is a combination of public and private partnerships . . . and programs to get into the supply chain. This is a management problem."[73]

A Coast Guard captain of the Port of San Francisco feels very strongly that, in time, the sea borders will be very secure—as long as everyone remains watchful. "After the *Exxon Valdez* [oil spill disaster] we became more responsive to oil spills," he explains. "It's similar with the terror threat. There are lots of challenges out there—prevention, coordination of effort. We're just beginning to understand the threat, and to respond."[74]

Chapter Five

The Changing Face of Immigration

The attacks of September 11 made many Americans fearful, but they also made people angry. Hearing that the terrorists were Middle Eastern immigrants who had legally obtained visas or other documentation to enter the United States only increased this outrage, for it showed how easily the nation had been duped, and how their own immigration system had been used against them. The INS was the target of much of the anger; but as Americans were told that there were most likely other terrorist cells operating within U.S. borders, immigrants themselves became targets.

"I Hated Everything About Them"

Some Americans became resentful or suspicious of those of Middle Eastern descent around them, even though they never had felt that way before. Although her anger was short-lived, one twenty-three-year-old hair dresser recalls the fury she felt at the time. "I was so outraged that people from another country, who didn't even know the people in those buildings, could do something like that—kill so many people and ruin so many lives," she says. "I hated them, I hated their religion, I hated everything about them."[75]

She says that she surprised herself with the intensity of the anger she felt. "I'm not a quick-tempered person, but I

A Middle Eastern immigrant surveys the damage from a brick thrown through his storefront after the September 11 attacks. Many such immigrants were the victims of such backlash violence.

really learned what it felt like to have that kind of temper," she says. "My boss at the shop is from Egypt—she's a lovely woman, very fair, very smart. But I had trouble thinking of her in the same way for a while. It was like, I saw her and I thought of those terrorists. She's not even Muslim, but in my mind, she was Middle Eastern, and that's all I saw."[76]

Many Muslims told reporters that they expected such backlash. In fact, some acknowledged that one of their first thoughts after learning of the September 11 attacks was that they hoped the hijackers were not Muslims. Their fears were well-founded, for in the days immediately after the terrorist attacks, there were a number of hate crimes against Muslim or Middle Eastern immigrants in the United States. One gas station owner in Arizona was gunned down as he worked in his garden. Although he was not Muslim, he wore a turban which evidently made him a target for an angry passerby.

There were scores of other crimes reported, too. Some people were shot at or beaten, including several Muslim women who were wearing traditional head scarves. Muslim temples were targets, too; windows were broken and hate slogans were spray painted on walls and doors.

Some Muslim immigrants attempted to explain that their religion is supposed to be a very peaceful one, and assured people that they, too, were horrified by the attacks. Other Muslim or Middle Eastern immigrants, nervous that they might be blamed, avoided the subject altogether, or even pretended that they were from an entirely different part of the world. One New York City taxi driver from Bangladesh says that he turned the license in his cab around so that passengers could not see that his first name was Mohammed. To protect himself, he says, he had a ready answer when people asked him about his nationality. "I tell them [Bangladesh] is in South America," he shrugs. "And then they sort of relax."[77]

Keep the Borders Closed for a While

After the first emotional days after September 11, much of the violence against immigrants stopped. In fact, some Muslim immigrants reported that some people had apologized—either for their own rash behavior, or that of other Americans. "We had a lady who came in and didn't buy anything," says one Memphis gas station owner, a Pakistani immigrant. "She just wanted to check on us and see that we were okay. Another lady brought by a plant with a note that said she hoped that out of this we would all learn to live in peace."[78]

However, another type of trouble was not as fleeting. Rather than acts of violence directed at Muslims or Middle Eastern immigrants, there were cries from citizens and lawmakers for a formal policy change that would limit the number of immigrants and refugees who could be allowed in the United States. Steve, a Minneapolis banker, says that he was astounded at the large volume of people going through border checkpoints each year. He agreed that there should be dramatic cuts in the numbers of immigrants allowed to enter the country. "I think it's that we've got too many people coming and going," he says. "I think we should just keep the borders closed for a while. It sounds mean, but why should the United States put itself at risk by being everybody's destination?"[79]

But other Americans were not sure that limiting immigration was the answer. They pointed out that the United States had always been a welcoming country, a country made up primarily of immigrants. They wondered whether changing the way the United States viewed newcomers was the right thing to do. One Middle Eastern man who recently became a U.S. citizen insists that such a change would be a victory for al-Qaeda. "The greatest victory for Osama bin Laden, of course, would be if America lost faith in its openness," he says. "That is his goal."[80]

Denying visas or citizenship to people from the Middle East could break up immigrant families like this one in which only one parent is a citizen.

"Enforcement Is the Primary Responsibility"

Although the government did not declare an intent to deter immigrants from entering the United States, it did make a bureaucratic change. The Department of Homeland Security replaced the INS in handling immigration issues. The Bureau of Citizenship and Immigration Services became responsible for the welcoming aspects of immigration, while the Bureau of Immigration and Customs Enforcement dealt with problems such as managing those immigrants who have committed a crime, or tracking down the many thousands of immigrants who have overstayed their visas.

Though DHS officials said that the responsibility of servicing new immigrants was an important one, they admitted that fighting terrorism was their primary concern. "Yes, enforcement is the primary responsibility of this department," one spokesman says. "But this is a welcoming country that was created by immigrants. And we are going to do as much as we possibly can to make services more efficient and helpful to the immigrant community."[81]

However, many immigration advocates in the United States disapproved of the DHS's emphasis on enforcement. These advocates predicted that merely the act of incorporating the Bureau of Citizenship and Immigration Services into the DHS would send the wrong message to immigrants—especially recent arrivals who must struggle with 475 pages of new immigration rules, put into effect after September 11. "I think there's going to be total confusion," says an immigration attorney in Washington, D.C. "Our members are getting a lot of calls from immigrants who feel that they are the ones being isolated, not the terrorists."[82]

Delays

One of the new rules inspired by the terrorist attacks requires much more detailed background checks for anyone seeking to move to the United States. The goal, of course, is to

Ghassan Elashi (pictured) and his brothers were arrested on suspicion of supporting terrorism after September 11.

prevent suspected terrorists and criminals from entering the country. To accomplish this, U.S. officials overseas are required to run the names of every immigrant applicant against FBI databases, to fingerprint them, and to do more extensive interviews than ever before.

Although the number of people applying for immigration status did not drop after September 11, the speed at which the applications are processed has slowed considerably. Officials say that the additional requirements of "support documents"—various identification documents, such as birth and wedding certificates, for example—are slowing the processing time from a few months to well over a year. "I think there's just great pressure on immigration officials to check everything very thoroughly," says one immigration official, "and that slows down the whole process."[83]

Refugees, too, are facing long delays. For them the waiting can be very dangerous, for many face torture or death in their own countries. Many say that because of the violence or unrest in their countries, the documents now required by immigration officials are very hard to get. There has been a dramatic decrease in the number of refugees granted asylum since September 11. In 2002, there were 80 percent fewer arrivals of refugees.

Immigration authorities say that the decrease is due only to the shortage of U.S. personnel to interview and run document checks on the applicants, but some immigration advocates suspect there is a more devious explanation. One immigration counselor says, "According to my sources, with the new merger in immigration offices and all this security, things have become very tough for immigrants. Sometimes you think [the slowdown] is intentional because they don't want immigrants in the U.S."[84]

A Frayed Welcome Mat

There are also some questions about the new rules that apply to immigrants already in the United States. One law that has been very controversial was passed very soon after the terrorist attacks. Called the USA Patriot Act, it gives sweeping powers to the government to investigate and prevent terrorism. Under the Patriot Act, law enforcement agencies can detain any immigrant for as long as six months without a trial if he or she is suspected of being a terrorist. Under the act, the person does not automatically have attorney-client privileges, nor does any evidence against the person need to be explained or revealed.

In many cases, the FBI would do large sweeps of an area—almost always one that is heavily Muslim or Middle Eastern—and arrest and question hundreds or even thousands of immigrants. Many Americans have criticized the extensive new powers of the government, and expressed shock that the civil liberties of so many people were being ignored. Immigration advocates complained that the United States was quickly turning into a place where all people entering as immigrants were suspected of being terrorists.

And while some immigrants say that they understood why the government was anxious to interrogate Muslims and Middle Eastern people, they also were uncomfortable at being suspected of terrorism. "Many of us left our homes to begin with because of terrorism," says one Palestinian woman who has lived in the United States for eight years. "The last thing we want to have here is the kind of terrorism that our relatives see almost daily," she says. "That would be horrible."[85]

"None of Us Knows Where That Line Is"

When the arrests and detentions first began, few immigrants complained, however. They worried that to protest being targeted might further anger intelligence or law enforcement officers. An official of the American Muslim Council agreed that complaints to the authorities were rare. While civil rights are important, few Muslims want to appear unsympathetic with the nation's need to be safe. "There's a line between our desire for security and for civil liberties," he said. "Right now none of us knows where that line is."[86]

But some Americans say they know exactly where that line is. They insist that any time a certain ethnic or religious group is profiled for such treatment, the government is overstepping its bounds. "I read a newspaper article about people being 'detained,'" says Susan, a special education teacher. "I remember the word sounds so polite, as though 'detaining' was simply an unavoidable little mix-up or something. But it sounded so premeditated. I wonder if Americans in the Middle East would be willing to be detained if officials there ordered it."[87]

Newsweek editor Fareed Zakaria, an immigrant from India, disagrees with the method of interrogation—not

because of its violation of civil rights, but because it alienates the immigrant community when the intelligence agencies most need their cooperation. He tells about an Arab artist who was detained by the FBI. After putting him in a cell and interrogating him for three hours, the man was insulted by agents who called him names. He slept on the concrete floor with two other detainees, not knowing how long he would be kept in the cell. The following morning, however, the FBI agents had changed their approach. They told him that they believed him, and would like him to work with the FBI, helping them translate when they did other such interviews. "Guess what?" Zakaria asks. "He declined."[88]

Agreeing that they found the provisions of the new laws to be excessive, some town councils passed resolutions calling the USA Patriot Act a threat to immigrants

U.S. soldiers search the home of an immigrant suspected of possible terrorist connections. Many citizens condemn such searches as a violation of civil rights.

in their communities. In Cambridge, Massachusetts, for example, the resolution stated, "We believe these civil liberties [freedom of speech, assembly, and privacy; equality before the law; due process; and freedom from unreasonable searches and seizures] are now threatened by the U.S.A. Patriot Act."[89]

Attorney General John Ashcroft, however, insists that the uncertain times warrant extra suspicion of Middle Eastern and Muslim people, especially young men. Ashcroft has warned U.S. citizens against even discussing the violations of civil liberty, insisting that such talk would merely cloud what he says is the most important issue—fighting terrorists.

"I Can See People Frown"

Some immigrants and their advocates say that it is hardly surprising that people are rarely open to helping law enforcement after they have received poor treatment themselves based on their ethnicity, religion, or race. Some feel that while terrorism is abhorrent, the idea of helping police officers who clearly do not respect immigrants is also unpleasant. Others feel that the United States has provided them with freedoms they never would have had in their native countries. For that reason, they say that they owe a debt of cooperation to police and intelligence agencies—whether they are treated well or not.

Mustafa, an immigrant from Ethiopia, says that he feels indebted, though he also feels that the United States needs to be more trustful of people. "I came here from a refugee camp nine years ago," he says. "A church here in the city sponsored me, and different people helped me when I got here. And before the terrorist hijackers, no one treated me like a criminal. But they do now. I look like a black American man, but the minute I start talking, I can see people frown. They never did that before. I can tell they are thinking, 'I wonder where this one, this man, is from?'"[90]

Registering

While various government agencies have worked to locate other terrorists among immigrant communities, the newly formed Bureau of Immigration and Customs Enforcement has been dealing with one of the INS's biggest problems— the hundreds of thousands of immigrants whose visas have run out, but who have remained in the country.

Once a student or work visa expires, immigrants are sent a letter notifying them that they must leave the country, for they are no longer here legally. However, approximately 355,000 people over the years have simply ignored these letters, or have moved without telling authorities (a violation of immigration rules) and have not received their letters. Before September 11, the INS had neither the manpower nor the motivation to track them down. Since the attacks, however, the government is very interested in those immigrants—especially those from countries that support terrorism.

Early in December 2002, the government announced a massive effort to register immigrants from such countries. By December 16, 2002, all immigrant men and boys from Sudan, Syria, Iraq, Iran, or Libya were required to register at an immigration office. Those from an additional thirteen nations were given a later deadline, and other immigrants from other nations have been gradually added to the list. Those who did not comply faced deportation.

"The Bottom Line"

Since the program began in December 2002, over 130,000 immigrants have been registered—a process that involves fingerprinting, an extensive interview, and the entering of all the information into a computer system. Officials say that in the process of registering immigrants, they have caught 11 men suspected of having terrorist connections, as well as 9,000 illegal aliens. In addition, they say that the information they have been given has helped them in fighting terrorism.

Government authorities have been happy about the program and its results so far, and acknowledge that it took a tragedy such as September 11 to show how vulnerable the United States has been because of a lack of effective immigration enforcement. "The bottom line is to protect the safety of the American people," says one Justice Department official. "This program has already showed us how effective we can be at maintaining an adequate system of border control."[91]

It has been criticized by others as discriminatory because the vast majority of immigrants ordered to register are Muslims. "This is clearly tarring a whole commuity with indelible ink," says one immigration advocate, "and it will make them much less likely to come forward with intelligence information we need from them." The Council on American-Islamic Relations likened the move to "asking Muslims to don star-and-crescent [a symbol of Islam] armbands, just as the Nazis required Jews to wear Stars of David during World War II."[92]

One twenty-three-year-old Pakistani immigrant worries that, by registering, he might be in danger of losing his student visa. "If I go to register, what if they arrest me?" he wonders. "I hear they are trying to arrest people, and I'm just scared that they will frame people. I'm scared for my life. . . . My college career is probably ruined. If they deport me, my life is in even bigger danger."[93]

"They're Using Us as an Example"

Those immigrants found to be absconders—those who have moved and ignored the government's letters to return to their native country—are arrested. One Sudanese immigrant who was taken into custody was surprised, for like many immigrants whose visas have expired, he believed that the government bureaucracy would not catch up with him. A judge told him in 1996 that he must return to Sudan, but he says that he ignored the order.

"I came to New York City," he admits. "I didn't give them my address." Immigration officials found him, however, and arrested him recently. "They knocked on the door," he says. "They said, 'Nobody move.' They handcuffed me, put me in a car. They said, 'You have a deport order on you.'"[94]

An American Muslim leader addresses a convention in December 2002. Many Muslim groups publicly protested the new immigrant registration policy.

Many of the absconders have been in the United States for many years, and have children who were born here. Safouh Hamoui, a Syrian immigrant, runs a grocery store in Seattle. He and his wife and three children were arrested at gunpoint at their suburban Seattle home in March 2003. Hamoui's twenty-year-old daughter was furious. "It seems we were caught up in a 9/11 mixup," she says, "but it's not fair. Who are they going after—a 52-year-old man who's trying to make a living for his family? They're using us as an example just because of the religion we practice."[95]

North to Canada

Some immigrants may apply for asylum, allowing them to remain in the United States. Others may ask for time to seek an extension of their visas. However, many immigrants whose visas have lapsed have been frightened to register. In increasing numbers, they have been fleeing to Canada where they are seeking refugee status.

Interestingly, not all of those fleeing to Canada are in the United States illegally. Many are nervous about registering for other reasons. For instance, one young man says that his father works for a news service at the United Nations, and has been publicly critical of the U.S. position in the Middle East. He worries that even though his student visa is current, the government will deport him as a way of retaliation.

Another says that the attitude of Americans toward immigrants since September 11 has changed, and he feels unsafe taking a chance by registering. "It's too dangerous to stay," he says. "I'm too frightened by the mood in the U.S. Until 9/11, Americans had a tolerance for people who work hard. Even if [we] were technically breaking some law of immigration or legal residency, no one cared. But now, I am too afraid of arrest and deportation. America is so full of hatred and vengeance toward Muslims. So I come to Canada, a more humanitarian place."[96]

But while Canada has been less stringent in the past about its requirements for new immigrants, a new agreement between the United States and Canada will change that. Early in 2003, the two nations agreed that Canada would soon begin to send immigrants back to the United States for registration. But until that process starts, they are flocking to the border by the hundreds.

"When we came [to America] the congratulations didn't stop for two months," says one Middle Eastern immigrant sadly. He understands why the United States is being careful, but feels that his dream of raising his two small children in America has been dashed. His visa is up for renewal, but he knows that because he is Muslim there is little chance, saying, "This is a very bad and very terrible finish."[97]

Conclusion

The Future of the Nation's Borders

Although there have been some important changes in the way America's borders are being secured, there is much more to be done. For example, government officials say that while the scrutiny of Muslims and Middle Eastern immigrants has been important since the September 11 attacks, they are hoping that in the not-too-distant future it will be possible to keep track of immigrants less conspicuously, and without appearing to single out any one group.

Better Documentation

One way this can be accomplished is to require all temporary visitors to the United States to have the same ID document. That would mean getting rid of the passport in its current form because they are easy for criminals to both obtain and to forge. After the terrorist attacks, it was discovered that several of the hijackers had entered the country using stolen or forged passports. In some cases, a valid passport is altered by changing the picture or biographical data to match the thief. In other cases, the passport is left as it is, in hopes that the border agent would be unable to notice the difference between the picture and the carrier.

Since December 2002, at thirty points along the U.S.-Mexican border, agents have been experimenting with a special new identificaion card for people entering the country. Resembling a driver's license or credit card, the card is called a biometric ID, which means that a 1.4-inch metallic strip at the bottom contains encrypted information, such as a digital photograph and an image of the cardholder's fingerprint. As the cardholder puts a finger on a special scanner, a machine "reads" the fingerprint and the encrypted information, making sure the two match.

Border agents using the new system have apprehended 150 people trying to enter by using another's card. In a case that most impressed inspectors a woman was caught using her twin sister's card—a catch that would never have happened with a traditional ID card.

"A Tiny Hard Drive"

Some security companies see these cards as a mere beginning. One company is experimenting with a card that contains a second memory strip which can store 20MB (megabytes) of data, roughly the capacity of fourteen floppy disks, says one technology expert, "essentially giving the card a tiny hard drive."[98] The data contained on this strip would be iris scans (the iris of a person's eye is as individual as a fingerprint), facial scans, medical data, and even DNA sequences. In addition, the cardholder's criminal record or known associations with terrorist groups could be included.

Another improvement envisioned for the future is making the card even more tamperproof by embedding a microscopic radio frequency chip and antenna within the photograph on the card. If a terrorist or other criminal attempted to alter the photo, the chip and antenna would be disturbed, and would alert the border agent when the card is put into a reader.

Not surprisingly, the idea of storing a great deal of data on individuals has provoked much debate among citizens and immigrants alike. One immigrant says that while the information could make the ID cards tamperproof, there is no guarantee that the data contained inside the card would be accurate. "What if they get me mixed up with a man who is a murderer?" he wonders. "What if they have the wrong fellow? Then who do I appeal to as I am standing in line at the airport with a machine buzzing at me? I think it is a mistake."[99]

Hidden Cameras and Flying Saucers

Less controversial are some ideas for patrolling the nation's land borders. At the onset of the war on terrorism in Afghanistan, the U.S. military used unmanned aircraft for reconnaissance, which greatly reduced the threat to troops. However, military experts said that the uninhabited aerial vehicles, or UAVs, are not always easy to use, especially because they can only be launched from a runway.

However, a new UAV has been tested in recent months which may be launched from almost anywhere. The UAV is very small—a little more than 14 feet across—and its shape looks

A Chinese official displays electronic ID cards to be issued to Chinese citizens. Americans may soon face similar high-tech security measures.

more like a flying saucer than an airplane. It would be equipped with cameras and computer equipment that could send up-to-the-minute images of the more likely spots for illegal crossing areas to border agents. Because it will be almost silent, the tiny UAV will be unnoticed by those who are trying to evade patrols.

High-tech infrared cameras, too, may soon be added to more of the remote points on the U.S.-Canadian border. They are expensive, but Department of Homeland Security officials believe that the more eyes and ears—even nonhuman ones—at the border, the safer the nation will be.

An Impossible Goal?

Robert Bonner, commissioner of Customs and Border Protection, is confident that the billions of dollars being spent by the department is a very good sign that the nation is taking border security seriously. "Technology is our greatest ally in preventing terrorists from getting weapons of mass destruction across our borders," he says. "It is technology that is allowing us to facilitate the movement of goods and people, while simultaneously giving us the capacity to detect weapons of mass destruction."[100]

But while many agree that the increased technology is making a difference in the ability of border and immigration agents to do a more effective job, some have doubts. Consumer advocate and 2000 presidential candidate Ralph Nader worries that too much money is being used on detectors and machines. "We could spend our entire gross national product on security," he says. "I mean, there is an infinite demand, right? Look how much we can spend searching every truck and vehicle that comes from Mexico. So we have to realize that there are some limits. While you can reduce some risks, avoid some risks, mostly we have got to be alert."[101]

Balancing the need for national security with important questions about privacy, openness, and civil liberties may be a task just as challenging—and every bit as important—as any that the nation has faced in the war on terrorism.

Notes

Introduction: "What Were We *Doing*?"

1. Personal interview, Rick, March 18, 2003, Edina, MN.

2. Personal interview, Susan, April 18, 2003, Minneapolis.

3. Quoted in Elisabeth Bumiller, "In Preview of State of the Union Message, Bush Calls for More Money for Border Patrols," *New York Times*, January 26, 2002, p. A9.

Chapter 1: The End of the INS

4. Eric Schmitt, "Agency Finds Itself Under Siege," *New York Times*, March 15, 2002, p. A11.

5. Personal interview, Jim, September 30, 2001, St. Paul, MN.

6. Personal interview, Gilda, October 11, 2001, St. Paul, MN.

7. Telephone interview, Joe, March 13, 2003.

8. Personal interview, Wayne, October 2, 2001, Minneapolis.

9. Quoted in Tim Weiner, "Border Customs Agents Are Pushed to the Limit," *New York Times*, July 25, 2002, p. A14.

10. Quoted in Bill Sapoito, "Deporting the INS," *Time*, March 25, 2002, p. 46.

11. Quoted in Schmitt, "Agency Finds Itself Under Siege," p. A11.

12. Quoted in Schmitt, "Agency Finds Itself Under Siege," p. A11.

13. Telephone interview, Clare, March 31, 2003.

14. Clare, March 31, 2003.

15. Personal interview, Ram, April 1, 2003, Edina, MN.

16. Quoted in Philip Shenon, "Investigators Entered U.S. with Fake Names and IDs," *New York Times*, January 21, 2003, p. A13.

17. Quoted in Jerry Seper, "140 More Agents Will Be Sent to Border," *Washington Times*, March 20, 2003, p. A4.

Chapter 2: The Economic and Political Faces of the Border

18. Steve Lohr, "How to Keep Cargo Safe, and Rolling," *New York Times*, May 27, 2002, p. C3.

19. Quoted in Kevin McCory, "Improved Security to Hasten Border Checks," *USA Today*, April 16, 2002, p. B1.

20. Quoted in Weiner, "Border Customs Agents Are Pushed to the Limit," p. A14.

21. Quoted in Barnard Simon, "A Border Giveth, and Taketh Away," *New York Times*, April 11, 2002, p. W1.

22. Quoted in Geri Smith, "Mending Fences South of the Border," *The America's Intelligence Wire*, April 7, 2003.

23. Quoted in Tim Weiner, "U.S. and Mexico Coordinate Military Efforts for Mutual Protection Against Terror," *New York Times*, March 23, 2003, p. B13.

24. Quoted in Weiner, "U.S. and Mexico Coordinate Military Efforts for Mutual Protection Against Terror," p. B13.

25. Quoted in Stephanie Handelman, "Border Guardian," *Time International*, December 31, 2001, p. 64.

26. Quoted in Handelman, "Border Guardian," p. 64.

27. Quoted in Handelman, "Border Guardian," p. 64.

28. Quoted in Elaine Shannon, "Manning the Bridge," *Time*, September 9, 2002, p. 102.

29. Quoted in Shannon, "Manning the Bridge," p. 104.

30. Personal interview, Bob, March 23, 2003, Minneapolis.

31. Quoted in Colin Campbell, "Delays Are Rare at U.S. Airports," *New York Times*, March 27, 2003, p. W1.

32. Quoted in Paul Levy, "Heightened Alert Could Mean More Travel Time," *StarTribune*, May 22, 2003, p. 1A.

33. Quoted in Jerry Seper, "Customs Chief Makes Pledge to Revamp Border Security," *Washington Times*, February 21, 2003, p. A12.

Chapter 3: The Human Borders

34. Quoted in Susan Catto, "Tighter Border Security Slows Canadian Traffic," *New York Times*, April 6, 2003, p. 3.

35. Personal interview, Pat, April 27, 2003, Lakeland, MN.

36. Quoted in Sarah Schweitzer, "Border Arrest Fuels Canada Ire Over U.S. Security," *Knight Ridder/Tribune Business News*, November 26, 2002.

37. Quoted in Eric Beaudan, "Restrictions Grow Along U.S.-Canada Line," *Christian Science Monitor*, November 29, 2002, p. 9.

38. Quoted in Schweitzer, "Border Arrest Fuels Canada Ire Over U.S. Security."

39. Telephone interview, Walt, April 30, 2003.

40. Quoted in Kevin Michael Grace, "Uncle Sam Looks North," *The Report Newsmagazine*, December 12, 2002.

41. Quoted in Grace, "Uncle Sam Looks North."

42. Name withheld, May 24, 2003, Minneapolis.

43. Quoted in Grace, "Uncle Sam Looks North."

44. Quoted in Clifford Krauss, "On Border Ire, Canada Says: Blame U.S.," *New York Times*, November 8, 2002, p. A8.

45. Quoted in Grace, "Uncle Sam Looks North."

46. Personal interview, Alicia, February 1997, Minneapolis.

47. Personal interview, Ana, July 1999, Minneapolis.

48. Quoted in Kris Axtman, "Illegal Border Crossings Get Even Riskier," *Christian Science Monitor*, September 24, 2002, p. 3.

49. Name withheld, February 7, 2003, St. Paul, MN.

50. Name withheld, February 7, 2003, Hopkins, MN.

51. Quoted in Axtman, "Illegal Border Crossings Get Even Riskier," p. 3.

52. Quoted in Weiner, "Border Customs Agents Are Pushed to the Limit," p. A14.

53. Quoted in Michael Janofsky, "Border Agents on Lookout for

Terrorists Are Finding Drugs," *New York Times*, March 6, 2002, p. A14.

54. Quoted in Ralph Vartabedian, "The Law Loses Out at U.S. Parks," *Los Angeles Times*, January 23, 2003, p. A1.

55. Quoted in Kelly P. O'Meara, "Civilians Patrolling the Border," *Insight on the News*, February 4, 2003, p. 18.

56. Telephone interview, Earle, May 5, 2003.

57. Earle, May 5, 2003.

Chapter 4: Securing America's Sea Borders

58. Quoted in Joel Brinkley, "Tinderbox of a Texas Port Points to a Threat by Sea," *New York Times*, March 5, 2002, p. A10.

59. Quoted in David Helvarg, "If by Sea," *Popular Science*, September 2002, p. 60.

60. Quoted in Allison Mitchell, "Where the Buffalo Roam Less," *New York Times*, January 20, 2002, p. A5.

61. Quoted in Brinkley, "Tinderbox of a Texas Port Points to a Threat by Sea," p. A10.

62. Quoted in Bob Port, "Nuclear Terrorism a Near-Term Threat," *Knight Ridder/Tribune News Service*, September 10, 2002.

63. John Mulligan, "Guarding Against Terrorists Is Job One for Coast Guard," *Providence Journal*, June 2, 2002, p. A1.

64. Quoted in Helvarg, "If by Sea," p. 61.

65. Quoted in Rusty Dornin, "Sea Marshals Ride Shotgun," CNN San Francisco, November 3, 2001. www.literacynet.org.

66. Quoted in Dornin, "Sea Marshals Ride Shotgun."

67. Quoted in Seth Schiesel, "Their Mission: Intercepting Deadly Cargo," *New York Times*, March 20, 2003, p. G1.

68. Personal interview, name withheld, March 23, 2003, Minneapolis.

69. Quoted in Helvarg, "If by Sea," p. 66.

70. Quoted in Michael Milligan, "Bill Addresses Port Security," *Travel Weekly*, April 14, 2003, p. 20.

71. Quoted in Angela Greiling Keane, "Show Ports the Money," *Traffic World*, April 21, 2003, p. 32.

72. Quoted in Mulligan, "Guarding Against Terrorists Is Job One for Coast Guard," p. A1.

73. Quoted in Christian Bourge, "Coast Guard Has New Mission," *Insight on the News*, September 2, 2002, p. 33.

74. Quoted in Helvarg, "If by Sea," p. 67.

Chapter 5: The Changing Face of Immigration

75. Personal interview, Pam, September 29, 2001. Minneapolis.

76. Pam, September 29, 2001.

77. Quoted in Nancy Gibbs, "Life on the Homefront," *Time*, October 1, 2001, p. 17.

78. Quoted in Tommy Perkins, "Muslim Business Owners See Wrath, Support in Reactions," *Memphis Business Journal*, September 21, 2001, p. 8.

79. Personal interview, Steve, March 1, 2003, Minneapolis.

80. Quoted in Fareed Zakaria, "An Immigrant's Faith," *Newsweek Commemorative Issue*, p. 87.

81. Quoted in Philip Shenon, "For Immigrants, the Watchword Suddenly Is Enforcement," *New York Times*, December 8, 2002, p. A4.

82. Quoted in Shenon, "For Immigrants, the Watchword Suddenly Is Enforcement," p. A4.

83. Quoted in Jack Chang, "Immigration Process Slowed with Security Checks," *Knight Ridder/Tribune News Service*, May 6, 2003.

84. Quoted in Chang, "Immigration Process Slowed with Security Checks."

85. Personal interview, Cassira, April 5, 2003, St. Paul, MN.

86. Quoted in Lynette Clemetson and Keith Naughton, "Patriotism vs. Ethnic Pride: An American Dilemma," *Newsweek*, September 24, 2001, p. 69.

87. Telephone interview, Susan, May 27, 2003.

88. Fareed Zakaria, "Freedom vs. Security," *Newsweek*, July 8, 2002, p. 26.

89. Quoted in Dean Schaber, "Patriot Revolution?" *abcNews.com*, July 1, 2002. www.abcnews.go.com.

90. Personal interview, Mustafa, May 1, 2003, Minneapolis.

91. Quoted in Rachel L. Swarns, "Fearful, Angry or Confused, Muslim Immigrants Register," *New York Times*, April 25, 2003, p. A1.

92. Quoted in Jodie Morse, "A Flap About Fingerprints," *Time*, June 17, 2002, p. 27.

93. Quoted in Brian Donohue, "9/11 Fallout Has Pakistanis Seeking Haven in Canada," Free Republic.com, January 8, 2003. www.forums5.aclu.org.

94. Quoted in Barry Newman, "U.S. Gets Tough on Deportees Who Abscond," *Wall Street Journal*, April 25, 2003, p. B1.

95. Quoted in Susan Sachs, "U.S. Begins Crackdown on Muslims Who Defy Orders to Leave Country," *New York Times*, April 2, 2002, p. A13.

96. Quoted in "Asylum Seekers Dash for Border," *WorldNetDaily*, January 4, 2003. www.worldnetdaily.com.

97. Quoted in Brian Donohue, "Pakistanis Piling Up at Exit Points to Canada," *Newhouse News Service*, March 11, 2003. www.new housenews.com.

Conclusion: The Future of the Nation's Borders

98. "Your ID Please, Citizen," *Popular Science*, September 2002, p. 77.

99. Telephone interview, Faroq, March 3, 2003.

100. Quoted in Schiesel, "Their Mission: Intercepting Deadly Cargo," p. G1.

101. "Can Science Make Us More Secure?" *Popular Science*, September 2002, p. 69.

For Further Reading

Books

Kathryn Gay, *Silent Death*. Brookfield, CT: Twenty-first Century Books, 2001. A very inclusive look at chemical and biological weapons, and how they might be used by terrorist groups.

Mary Williams, ed. *Terrorist Attack on America*. San Diego: Greenhaven Press, 2003. Good essays about the profiling of immigrants by law enforcement, as well as the balance between civil liberties and security.

Websites

U.S. Department of Homeland Security (www.dhs.gov). This site has various types of information—from breaking news to feature articles about how the border agencies work.

U.S. Coast Guard (www.uscg.mil). This site has history, current stories about port security and the vehicles used by the Coast Guard, and information on the changing role of the agency since September 11.

U.S. Immigration Service (www.usaimmigrationservice.org). From explanations of various work visas and necessary documentation, this site can show a reader how complex the system of immigration can be.

Works Consulted

Periodicals

Kris Axtman, "Illegal Border Crossings Get Even Riskier," *Christian Science Monitor*, September 24, 2002.

Eric Beaudan, "Restrictions Grow Along U.S.-Canada Line," *Christian Science Motor*, November 29, 2002.

Christian Bourge, "Coast Guard Has New Mission," *Insight on the News*, September 2, 2002.

Joel Brinkley, "Tinderbox of a Texas Port Points to a Threat by Sea," *New York Times*, March 5, 2002.

Elisabeth Bumiller, "In Preview of State of the Union Message, Bush Calls for More Money for Border Patrols," *New York Times*, January 26, 2002.

Colin Campbell, "Delays Are Rare at U.S. Airports," *New York Times*, March 27, 2003.

Susan Catto, "Tighter Border Security Slows Canadian Traffic," *New York Times*, April 6, 2003.

Jack Chang, "Immigration Process Slowed with Security Checks," *Knight Ridder/Tribune News Service*, May 6, 2003.

Lynette Clemetson and Keith Naughton, "Patriotism vs. Ethnic Pride: An American Dilemma," *Newsweek*, September 24, 2001.

Nancy Gibbs, "Life on the Homefront," *Time*, October 1, 2001.

Kevin Michael Grace, "Uncle Sam Looks North," *The Report Newsmagazine*, December 12, 2002.

Stephanie Handelman, "Border Guardian," *Time International*, December 31, 2001.

David Helvarg, "If by Sea," *Popular Science*, September 2002.

Michael Janofsky, "Border Agents on Lookout for Terrorists Are Finding Drugs," *New York Times*, March 6, 2002.

Angela Greiling Keane, "Show Ports the Money," *Traffic World*, April 21, 2003.

Clifford Krauss, "On Border Ire, Canada Says: Blame U.S.," *New York Times*, November 8, 2002.

Paul Levy, "Heightened Alert Could Mean More Travel Time," *StarTribune*, May 22, 2003.

Steve Lohr, "How to Keep Cargo Safe, and Rolling," *New York Times*, May 27, 2002.

Kevin McCory, "Improved Security to Hasten Border Checks," *USA Today*, April 16, 2002.

Michael Milligan, "Bill Addresses Port Security," *Travel Weekly*, April 14, 2003.

Allison Mitchell, "Where the Buffalo Roam Less," *New York Times*, January 20, 2002.

Jodie Morse, "A Flap About Fingerprints," *Time*, June 17, 2002.

John Mulligan, "Guarding Against Terrorists Is Job One for Coast Guard," *Providence Journal*, June 2, 2002.

Barry Newman, "U.S. Gets Tough on Deportees Who Abscond," *Wall Street Journal*, April 25, 2003.

Kelly P. O'Meara, "Civilians Patrolling the Border," *Insight on the News*, February 4, 2003.

Tommy Perkins, "Muslim Business Owners See Wrath, Support in Reactions," *Memphis Business Journal*, September 21, 2001, p. 8.

Popular Science, "Can Science Make Us More Secure?" September 2002.

————, "Your ID Please, Citizen," September 2002.

Bob Port, "Nuclear Terrorism a Near-Term Threat," *Knight Ridder/Tribune News Service*, September 10, 2002.

Susan Sachs, "U.S. Begins Crackdown on Muslims Who Defy Orders to Leave Country," *New York Times*, April 2, 2002.

Bill Sapoito, "Deporting the INS," *Time*, March 25, 2002.

Seth Schiesel, "Their Mission: Intercepting Deadly Cargo," *New York Times*, March 20, 2003.

Eric Schmitt, "Agency Finds Itself Under Siege," *New York Times*, March 15, 2002.

Sarah Schweitzer, "Border Arrest Fuels Canada Ire Over U.S. Security," *Knight Ridder/Tribune Business News*, November 26, 2002.

Jerry Seper, "Customs Chief Makes Pledge to Revamp Border Security," *Washington Times*, February 21, 2003.

———, "140 More Agents Will Be Sent to Border," *Washington Times*, March 20, 2003.

Elaine Shannon, "Manning the Bridge," *Time*, September 9, 2002.

Philip Shenon, "For Immigrants, the Watchword Suddenly Is Enforcement," *New York Times*, December 8, 2002.

———, "Investigators Entered U.S. with Fake Names and IDs," *New York Times*, January 21, 2003.

Barnard Simon, "A Border Giveth, and Taketh Away," *New York Times*, April 11, 2002.

Geri Smith, "Mending Fences South of the Border," *The America's Intelligence Wire*, April 7, 2003.

Rachel L. Swarns, "Fearful, Angry or Confused, Muslim Immigrants Register," *New York Times*, April 25, 2003.

Ralph Vartabedian, "The Law Loses Out at U.S. Parks," *Los Angeles Times*, January 23, 2003.

Tim Weiner, "Border Customs Agents Are Pushed to the Limit," *New York Times*, July 25, 2002.

———, "U.S. and Mexico Coordinate Military Efforts for Mutual Protection Against Terror," *New York Times*, March 23, 2003.

Fareed Zakaria, "Freedom vs. Security," *Newsweek*, July 8, 2002.

———, "An Immigrant's Faith," *Newsweek Commemorative Issue*.

Internet Sources

"Asylum Seekers Dash for Border," *WorldNetDaily*, January 4, 2003. www.worldnetdaily.com.

Brian Donohue, "9/11 Fallout Has Pakistanis Seeking Haven in Canada," Free Republic.com, January 8, 2003. www.forums5. aclu.org.

————, "Pakistanis Piling Up at Exit Points to Canada," *Newhouse News Service*, March 11, 2003. www.newhousenews.com.

Rusty Dornin, "Sea Marshals Ride Shotgun," CNN San Francisco, November 3, 2001. www.literacynet.org.

Dean Schaber, "Patriot Revolution?" *abcNews.com*, July 1, 2002. www.abcnews.go.com.

Index

Picture Credits

Cover Photo: © AP/Wide World Photos

© AFP/CORBIS, 31

© AFP/Getty Images, 66

© AP/Wide World Photos, 11, 16, 18, 19, 23, 25, 34, 37, 39, 41, 44, 46, 50, 51, 54, 56, 59, 65, 72, 74, 76, 81, 88

© Rebecca Cook/Reuters/Landov, 38

© CORBIS, 61

Department of Defense ARMY and NAVY, 79

© Jonathan Drake/Reuters/Landov, 63

© Eddie Rios/Bloomberg News/Landov, 28

© David Turnley/CORBIS, 14

About the Author

Gail B. Stewart received her undergraduate degree from Gustavus Adolphus College in St. Peter, Minnesota. She did her graduate work in English, linguistics, and curriculum study at the College of St. Thomas and the University of Minnesota. She taught English and reading for more than ten years.

She has written more than 145 books for young people, including a series for Lucent Books called The Other America. She has written many books on historical topics such as World War I and the Warsaw Ghetto.

Stewart and her husband live in Minneapolis with their three sons, Ted, Elliot, and Flynn; two dogs; and a cat. When she is not writing, she enjoys reading, walking, and watching her sons play soccer.